MULTICULTURAL EDUCATIO

James A. Banks, *Series Editor*

Multicultural Education, Transformative Knowledge, and Action:
Historical and Contemporary Perspectives
JAMES A. BANKS, Editor

Educating Citizens in a Multicultural Society
JAMES A. BANKS

We Can't Teach What We Don't Know:
White Teachers, Multiracial Schools
GARY HOWARD

Reducing Prejudice and Stereotyping in Schools
WALTER STEPHAN

The Light in Their Eyes:
Creating Multicultural Learning Communities
SONIA NIETO

Race and Culture in the Classroom:
Teaching and Learning Through Multicultural Education
MARY A. DILG

Reducing Prejudice and Stereotyping in Schools

WALTER STEPHAN

FOREWORD BY JAMES A. BANKS

Teachers College, Columbia University
New York and London

Published by Teachers College Press, 1234 Amsterdam Avenue, New York, NY 10027

Library of Congress Cataloging-in-Publication Data
Stephan, Walter G.
    Reducing prejudice and stereotyping in schools / Walter Stephan;
    foreword by James A. Banks.
      p.   cm. — (Multicultural education series)
    Includes bibliographical references (p.   ) and index.
    ISBN 0-8077-3811-5 (cloth : alk. paper)
    ISBN 0-8077-3810-7 (paper : alk. paper)
    1. School integration—United States.   2. Discrimination in
education—United States—Prevention   3. Prejudices—United States.
4. Stereotype (Psychology)—United States.   5. Intergroup
relations—United States.   6. Multicultural education—United
States.   I. Title.   II. Series: Multicultural education series (New
York, N.Y.)
    LC214.2 .S74 1999
    306.43′2—dc21   98-47219

ISBN 0-8077-3810-7 (paper)
ISBN 0-8077-3811-5 (cloth)

Printed on acid-free paper
Manufactured in the United States of America

06 05 04 03 02 01 00 99   8 7 6 5 4 3 2 1

For Cookie

CONTENTS

Series Foreword *by James A. Banks*   ix
Introduction   xiii

CHAPTER 1   Stereotypes: Theory and Research   1
    A Network Model of Stereotypes   3
    Changing Stereotypes   17

CHAPTER 2   Prejudice: Theory and Research   24
    Theories of Prejudice   25
    Development of Intergroup Attitudes   33
    Implications of Theories of Prejudice for
       Changing Prejudice   34

CHAPTER 3   Contact Theory   40
    Contact Hypothesis   41
    Updated Contact Theory   46
    School Desegregation   50
    Insights from the Contact Model   55

CHAPTER 4   Improving Intergroup Relations   58
    Techniques Developed for Educational Settings   58
    Techniques Developed in Noneducational Settings   67
    Issues that Have an Impact on Intergroup Relations
       in the Schools   71
    Conclusion   76

CHAPTER 5   Recommendations for Intergroup Relations Programs   80
    Recommendations Relating to Social Information Processing   82
    Recommendations Relating to Value and Identity Issues   92

Recommendations Relating to Intergroup Relations Skills   96
Recommendations Relating to the Social Culture
    of the Schools   100

References   103
Index   133

SERIES FOREWORD

The nation's deepening ethnic texture, interracial tension and conflict, and the increasing percentage of students who speak a first language other than English make multicultural education an imperative as we enter a new century. The 1990 Census indicated that one of every four Americans is a person of color. About one out of every three Americans will be a person of color by the turn of the century.

American classrooms are experiencing the largest influx of immigrant students since the turn of the century. More than eight million legal immigrants settled in the United States between 1981 and 1990 (U.S. Bureau of the Census, 1994). A large but undetermined number of undocumented immigrants also enter the United States each year. The influence of an increasingly ethnically diverse population on the nation's schools, colleges, and universities is and will continue to be enormous. In 50 of the nation's largest urban public school systems, African-Americans, Latinos, Asian-Americans, and other students of color made up 76.5% of the student population in 1992 (Council of the Great City Schools, 1994). In some of the nation's largest cities and metropolitan areas, such as Chicago, Los Angeles, Washington, D.C., New York, Seattle, and San Francisco, half or more of the public school students are students of color. In California, the population of students of color in the public schools has exceeded the percentage of White students since the 1988–1989 school year.

Students of color will make up about 46% of the nation's student population by 2020 (Pallas, Natriello, and McDill, 1989). Fourteen percent of school-age youth live in homes in which English is not the first language (U. S. Bureau of the Census, 1994). Most teachers now in the classroom and in teacher education programs are likely to have students from diverse ethnic, cultural, and racial groups in their classrooms during their careers. This is true for both inner-city and suburban teachers.

An important goal of multicultural education is to improve race relations and to help all students acquire the knowledge, attitudes, and skills needed to participate in crosscultural interactions and in personal, social, and civic action that will help make our nation more democratic and just. Multicultural education is consequently as important for middle-class White suburban students as it is for students of color who live in the inner-city. Multicultural education fosters the public good and the overarching goals of the commonwealth.

The major purpose of the Multicultural Education Series is to provide preservice educators, practicing educators, graduate students, and scholars with an interrelated and comprehensive set of books that summarizes and analyzes important research, theory, and practice related to the education of ethnic, racial, cultural, and language groups in the United States and the education of mainstream students about ethnic and cultural diversity. The books in the Series provide research, theoretical, and practical knowledge about the behaviors and learning characteristics of students of color, language minority students, and low-income students. They also provide knowledge about ways to improve race relations in educational settings.

The definition of multicultural education in the *Handbook of Research on Multicultural Education* (Banks & Banks, 1995) is used in this Series: "multicultural education is a field of study designed to increase educational equity for all students that incorporates, for this purpose, content, concepts, principles, theories, and paradigms from history, the social and behavioral sciences, and particularly from ethnic studies and women studies" (p. xii). In the Series, as in the *Handbook,* multicultural education is considered a "metadiscipline."

The dimensions of multicultural education, developed by Banks (1995) and described in the *Handbook of Research on Multicultural Education,* provide the conceptual framework for the development of the books in the Series. They are: *content integration, the knowledge construction process, prejudice reduction, an equity pedagogy,* and *an empowering school culture and social structure.* To implement multicultural education effectively, teachers and administrators must attend to each of the five dimensions of multicultural education. They should use content from diverse groups when teaching concepts and skills, help students to understand how knowledge in the various disciplines is constructed, help students to develop positive intergroup attitudes and behaviors, and modify their teaching strategies so that students from different racial, cultural, and social-class groups will experience equal educational opportunities. The total environment and culture of the school must also be transformed so that students from diverse ethnic and cultural groups will experience equal status in the culture and life of the school.

Although the five dimensions of multicultural education are highly interrelated, each requires deliberate attention and focus. Each book in the series focuses on one or more of the dimensions, although each book deals with all of them to some extent because of the highly interrelated characteristics of the dimensions.

Students come to school with beliefs, attitudes, and values that reflect those of the communities in which they are being socialized and of the larger society. Many of the beliefs and attitudes that students have of different racial, ethnic, and cultural groups are based on stereotypes that are reinforced by representations of these groups in the mass media. Students also have experiences in the schools that reinforce their negative attitudes and beliefs about different racial and ethnic groups. Ability grouping which is stratified by race and class and teaching materials that privilege some groups over others are school practices that reinforce the ethnic and racial tension within the larger society.

This important, well-researched, and informative book was written by a sensitive and committed social psychologist who has spent much of his career doing research and writing about ways to improve race relations in classrooms and schools. It will help classroom teachers and other practicing educators to design and implement classroom interventions that will help students to develop more positive racial and ethnic attitudes and behaviors. This book is timely because the growth of diversity within the larger society and the schools is evoking nativism and intergroup conflict. In recent years much of this conflict has been manifested as attacks on second language instruction in the schools and on affirmative action policies. It is essential that intergroup tension and conflict be reduced as we re-imagine and reconstruct the U.S. for the new century. Educators will find this book invaluable as they seek the knowledge needed to reduce racial, ethnic, and cultural conflict in their schools.

James A. Banks

REFERENCES

Banks, J A. (1995). Multicultural education: Historical development, dimensions, and practice. In J. A. Banks & C. A. M. Banks (Eds.), *Handbook of research on multicultural education* (pp. 3–24). New York: Macmillan.

Banks, J. A. & Banks, C. A. M. (Eds.) (1995). *Handbook of research on multicultural education.* New York: Macmillan.

Council of the Great City Schools (1994). *National urban education goals: 1992–1993 Indicators report.* Washington, D.C.: Author.

Pallas, A. M., Natriello, G. & McDill, E. L. (1989). The changing nature of the disadvantaged population: Current dimensions and future trends. *Educational Researcher, 18* (5), 16–22.

United States Bureau of the Census (1994). *Statistical abstract of the United States* (114th edition). Washington, D.C.: U.S. Government Printing Office.

INTRODUCTION

I want to start this book by inviting the reader to think about two seemingly simple questions. What is prejudice and what are stereotypes? What does it mean to say that a person is prejudiced or that a person relies on stereotypes? I say that these questions are seemingly simple because all of us have an intuitive grasp of prejudice and stereotyping, but I would argue that the answers to these two questions are not simple; instead they are multifaceted and quite complex. Why are students prejudiced and why do they stereotype others? Are prejudice and stereotyping related to one another? Can they operate below the level of conscious awareness? How are the thoughts and feelings associated with prejudice and stereotyping organized and represented in our minds? Can prejudice co-exist with apparently contradictory attitudes such as sympathy and compassion? In what ways do prejudice and stereotypes affect how we think and feel about others? When are they activated and when are they dormant? What functions do stereotypes and prejudice serve, and how do the functions they serve nurture and sustain them?

Until we understand the answers to these questions we will not be a in strong position to ask if prejudice and stereotypes can be changed and how to go about changing them. Why is understanding the nature of stereotyping and prejudice so important for fashioning remedies? The fact that the simple remedies have been tried repeatedly and found wanting is perhaps the best indicator of the need for greater understanding. For instance, why does presenting students with information that disconfirms their stereotypes lead to such minimal changes? Why doesn't the intergroup contact that occurs in the schools reduce prejudice and stereotyping in so many cases? Why doesn't teaching our children that stereotyping and prejudice are wrong prevent them from becoming prejudiced and stereotyping others?

In the following pages I will review more than 500 studies on intergroup relations. Each of the authors has spent hundreds of hours researching and thinking about stereotyping and prejudice and ways of eliminating them. Many have dedicated their careers to this quest. In this book I will attempt to synthesize and summarize their theories and research (and some of my own) on stereotyping and prejudice. In addition, I will apply the knowledge we have obtained about the causes and nature of stereotypes and prejudice to formulate suggestions for reducing stereotyping and prejudice in school settings. I also will review the available research on programs designed specifically to eliminate stereotypes and reduce prejudice. I will end by making a series of concrete recommendations for how to improve intergroup relations in the schools.

The focus of my efforts will be on understanding stereotypes and prejudice as they exist in the minds of individuals. I will focus on changing individuals' beliefs (stereotypes) and attitudes (prejudice). I will be less concerned with how we can change the structural relations among various racial, ethnic, religious, or other groups that currently exist in our society. Obviously, there is a racial and ethnic hierarchy in this country, differences in social class do exist, and there are disparities in political and economic power among different groups. The intergroup relations that occur in our schools take place against the backdrop of the current structural relations between groups that exist in our society, and these structural factors clearly affect what happens in schools. Thus, we need to be aware of these effects and the roles they play in shaping intergroup relations in the schools. And we need to teach children about the pernicious effects of these structural relations among groups. However, this book will not be devoted to discussing ways of changing these structural relations, but instead will focus on changing the hearts and minds of individual members of all social groups. If we are successful in modifying intergroup relations in the schools, we also will contribute to changing the structural relations between groups in the long run. The institutions in our society are composed of individuals whose own socialization determines how they will act in the roles they come to occupy within these institutions. If the schools improve the intergroup relationship skills of the individuals who will work in these institutions, then improvements in intergroup relations at the structural, as well as the individual, level will occur. In short, my goal in this book is to examine what teachers can do in their classrooms to reduce stereotyping and prejudice.

The discussion that follows is sometimes technical, but it could not be otherwise and accurately portray the complexity and richness of the field. I can only hope that readers will not be tempted to skim over small, but potentially important, nuances in our understanding of these complicated issues.

I will begin by presenting a discussion of the nature of stereotypes. In these sections I will discuss basic research and theory concerning the structure and functioning of stereotypes. If we are to change stereotypes, we must understand exactly what they are and how they operate.

I wish to thank Cookie White Stephan, Brenda Sisson, Francis Aboud, Emily Isberg, and several anonymous reviewers, as well as the participants in the Cancun Conference, for their constructive feedback on the manuscript. I want to offer a special thank you to Jim Banks for his counsel and support. The writing of this book was supported in part by grants from the Carnegie Foundation.

Chapter 1

STEREOTYPES: THEORY AND RESEARCH

There is nothing as practical as a good theory.

—Lewin, 1944, p. 27

In one of the exercises I use in my class on intergroup relations, I ask my students if they have ever been the object of stereotyping. Last year, one of my students said that when she was in high school she submitted an essay to a national contest on what it meant to her to be an American. Her essay was selected as one of the 10 best in the country and she was flown to San Diego to be interviewed along with the other contestants. My student's mother is Mexican-American and her father is White, but she is quite dark skinned. All the other finalists were White. The selection committee questioned her about who wrote her essay and asked her for other samples of her writing. Despite her anger at the fact that only she was singled out for this treatment, she responded to their request. She felt humiliated. She did not win the contest. She believes that when the selection committee saw her, they decided that someone who looked so obviously Mexican-American could not have written such a fine essay herself. As she recounted this event, 3 years after it occurred, I could still see the pain on her face. Sticks and stones can break your bones, but stereotypes too can hurt you.

Stereotypes consist primarily of the traits attributed to social groups. In some respects, stereotypes are similar to the generalizations we all make about nonsocial categories (e.g., the characteristics of birds or trees). And, like these other generalizations, sometimes stereotypes are useful in everyday social interaction. For example, stereotypes provide us with expectations that can be used to guide our interactions with physicians, nurses, waitpersons, accountants, professors, infants, schizophrenics, depressed people, con-artists, shy people, and

1

so on. For intergroup relations, stereotypes are important because they so frequently have detrimental effects. Stereotypes of social groups are often negative, overgeneralized, and incorrect (Brigham, 1971; Stephan & Stephan, 1996a). When they are negative, they lead us to expect negative behaviors from outgroup members. When they are overgeneralized, they lead us to expect most outgroup members to behave in similar ways and they prevent us from treating outgroup members as individuals. When they are incorrect, they cause suffering to those who are misperceived and they lead to misunderstandings and conflict.

Because of their age, students seem to be particularly prone to rely on stereotypes as a shortcut to dealing with the complexities of the social world. The mass media, their family members, and their friends often furnish them with ready-made stereotypes that can be applied so the social groups in their environment. They come to believe that African-Americans are athletic, that Asian-Americans are smart, that Whites think they are superior, and a host of other misleading stereotypes. Worse yet, these stereotypes become the basis for their interactions with members of other groups, creating a variety of problems for both the students who use them and the members of the stereotyped groups. If they cause so much trouble, why are they so stubbornly retained?

One of the reasons that stereotypes are retained is that they serve so many functions, including helping people to maintain a positive self-image, justifying their social status and worldview (Jost & Banaji, 1993), reducing the complexity of the social world, and providing guidelines for social interaction. They also are retained because the ways in which they are structured and represented in people's minds make them difficult to change. To understand the manner in which stereotypes are structured we must first grasp the nature of the social categorization process.

The basis of stereotyping is categorization. When creating social categories, we focus on the characteristics that make the people in that category similar and that distinguish them from other people. Thus, when we categorize people by using a group label, we are highlighting the similarity of people within the category and the ways in which these people differ from other groups. To label people as Hispanic, handicapped, or homosexual is to emphasize the aspect of their identities that differentiates them from other people, while de-emphasizing the differences among the individual members of that group. For example, White students are likely to see African-American students as more different from Whites than they actually are and as more similar to one another than they actually are.

A NETWORK MODEL OF STEREOTYPES

Network models were created to help us understand how people organize and process information. They will be useful to us because they provide us with insights into how information about stereotypes of different groups (e.g., African-American, Asian-American, Hispanic, etc.) is stored in the mind. If we wish to change students' stereotypes, we first must understand how they operate and why they resist change. In network models, it is assumed that discrete bits of information, called *nodes*, are linked together to form networks. These networks create well-worn pathways in the mind that structure how we experience the social world. The more we use these pathways, the more ingrained they become—and the harder they are to change. As we will see, one of the great values of network models is that they tell us what has to be modified if we wish to reduce stereotyping. To jump ahead a bit, to change networks we must either alter the existing pathways or add new ones. But, before we can discuss changing stereotype networks, we need to thoroughly understand them.

Stereotypes can be described as a network of associated nodes of information (cf. Anderson, 1983; Rumelhart, Hinton, & McClelland, 1986) linking social groups to a whole constellation of other types of information. I will discuss five basic types of information (nodes) included in stereotype networks: defining features, group labels, characteristic features, behaviors, and exemplars (individual members of the group; see Figure 1.1).

The *defining features* of a social category consist of the criteria used to define group membership (Smith, Shoben, & Rips, 1974). For stereotypes, the defining features are the ones we use to categorize people as members of a given group. In their everyday lives, people tend to rely on physical appearance when making judgments concerning race and ethnicity, but the process is not always so simple. How do we decide that a person is an Asian-American? What if the person is of mixed Euro-American and Korean-American heritage? What if this person does not have the physical features thought to be associated with Asian-Americans? Whatever the features are that an individual uses to make such decisions, they are that individual's defining features. The defining features are closely related to the *group labels* we use in naming the groups—when we have defined a person as a member of a given group, we apply the relevant label to him or her.

The *characteristic features* do not define the category, but they are associated with the group label. The most important characteristic features of stereotypes consist of the traits associated with the category.

Figure 1.1. Network Model of Stereotypes

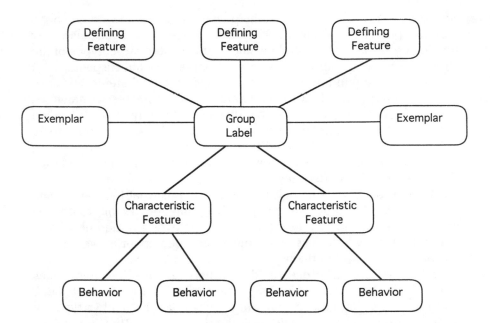

The defining and characteristic features of social categories are qualitatively different. To be identified as a category member, an individual must possess at least some of the defining features. However, an individual may possess none of the characteristic features of a category and still be a category member. For example, a person who is categorized as a Jew (because she possesses the defining characteristic of being born to a Jewish mother or having converted to Judaism), but who possesses none of the traits that are thought to be associated with the stereotype of Jewish people, is still considered to be a Jew. The links between group labels and characteristic features means that when students use racial epithets to refer to other students who are members of disliked groups, they are not only categorizing the other students, but they are also likely to attribute a set of personality traits (usually negative ones!) to the other students at the same time.

The *behaviors* of relevance to stereotypes are primarily those linked to the characteristic features (traits). Generally, we expect category members to behave in ways that are consistent with the traits associated with the category. For instance, we expect people who are thought to be aggressive to behave in aggressive ways.

Exemplars consist of individual members of the social category that the person has directly or indirectly encountered. For the ethnic category Americans of Japanese descent, the exemplars would consist of the particular Japanese-Americans that the individual knows, has read or heard about, or has seen in the media. Category exemplars are important in stereotyping because they may be used in forming stereotypes or making judgments about groups.

Studies indicate that information about ingroups (the groups to which we belong) is more likely to be processed in terms of exemplars, whereas information about outgroups (the groups of which we are not members) is more likely to be processed in terms of characteristic features—traits and other attributes (Ostrom, Carpenter, Sedikides, & Li, 1993). Thus, we tend to individualize ingroup members, while viewing outgroup members in terms of their traits and other characteristics. African-American students may see Whites in terms of their traits (deceitful, industrious, selfish, nervous, and conceited, according to one study) (Stephan & Rosenfield, 1982), but they see members of their own group as individuals (Kareem, Latisha, Michael, Janet, etc.). This emphasis on different processing strategies for ingroup and outgroup members is one of the many factors that facilitate the formation of stronger outgroup than ingroup stereotypes, and it makes outgroup stereotypes difficult to change.

Processing in Stereotype Networks

A stereotype network can be activated by events that occur in the external environment or by internal thought processes, such as consciously thinking about the group. When a node in a stereotype network becomes active, activation spreads outward along whatever links exist to other nodes. The flow of activation through networks is often completely automatic (Bargh, 1984, 1988). Thus, activation can be a passive process; it does not have to involve conscious awareness at all. The automatic activation of stereotypes can occur whenever we encounter members of stereotyped social groups (Devine, 1989). For example, the stereotype of Whites could be activated in the mind of an African-American student when a White student is encountered—without the African-American student even being aware of this activation. Of course, it is also possible for people to be consciously aware of processing stereotype information, as when an African-American student consciously thinks about his or her beliefs concerning White students.

Processing in stereotype networks typically begins with activation of the nodes for the defining features. Information about many defining features (e.g., skin color, clothing, language usage) is immediately available in many face-to-face social interactions. Activation then spreads automatically to the group node, and the person is categorized as a member of a given group. For instance, to activate the group node for "man," such defining features as the presence of masculine clothing, a (potentially) bearded face, and sex-appropriate nonverbal behavior or large physical size may have to be activated.

Next, activation spreads from the group node to the stereotype-related traits. Thus, the group node for "man" might activate the traits aggressiveness, coldness, lack of emotional expressiveness, and competitiveness in a person holding the traditional male stereotype (Spence & Helmreich, 1978). Activation also would spread to the associated behaviors, possibly leading the person to expect such behaviors as inhibition of emotional displays or engaging in competitive behavior during games.

Activation also can flow through the network in the other direction. The observation of behavior would activate nodes associated with these behaviors, which could, in turn, activate the related trait and group nodes. If you heard a person described as aggressive, cold, unemotional, and competitive, you might assume, without thinking much about it, that the person was a man because these traits are more strongly associated with men than with women in the gender stereotypes that exist in our culture.

When stereotype-related traits are activated, this activation subsequently can lead to more extreme ratings of members of the stereotyped group on that trait dimension (Banaji, Hardin, & Rothman, 1993). For example, in one study it was found that activating the trait "aggressive" subsequently led to more extreme ratings of men on this trait, but it did not affect the ratings of women (Banaji et al., 1993). In practice, this tendency means that once a stereotype is activated, people may be predisposed to make extreme stereotype-consistent evaluations of individuals from that group.

The strength of the links between the nodes in a network depends on the frequency and consistency with which the links have been activated (Bargh, 1988; Smith & Lerner, 1986). As a consequence of their greater frequency of use, the links running from the group node to the traits are probably stronger than the links running from the traits to the group node (cf. Andersen & Klatzky, 1987). Thus, when we identify a person as member of a given group, it is very likely to activate the corresponding stereotype; but when a stereotyped trait is activated, it may not activate the group node.

A brief research example will help to illustrate how networks function in stereotyping. In this study, a telephone survey was conducted with White respondents chosen at random from residents of Lexington, Kentucky (Sniderman, Tetlock, Carmines, & Peterson, 1993). They were asked to respond to questions concerning the stereotype of African-Americans (arrogant, irresponsible, lazy, and violent, in this study) either before or after they were asked to respond to questions regarding affirmative action programs favoring African-Americans. It was found that African-Americans were stereotyped to a much greater degree (on three of the four traits) if the affirmative action questions preceded, rather than followed, the questions regarding the stereotypes of African-Americans. From a network perspective, it appears that asking questions about affirmative action activated the group node for African-Americans and, as a result, the negative stereotypes of African-Americans also were activated. The activation of the stereotyped traits probably occurred automatically and was outside of conscious awareness. When the stereotype questions were posed, the negative stereotypes of African-Americans were already accessible and therefore more negative traits were attributed to African-Americans.

Implications of Associative Network Models for Stereotypes

> The self-fulfilling prophecy is, in the beginning, a false definition of the situation evoking a new behavior which makes the originally false conception come true. The specious validity of the self-fulfilling prophecy perpetuates a reign of error. (Merton, 1948, p. 195)

Activating stereotypes can set in motion a sequence of related events that confirms the stereotype. This expectancy-confirmation sequence has three stages, beginning with the collection of information that confirms the stereotype, proceeding to the biased processing of confirming and disconfirming information, and culminating in behavior that will cause the stereotype-based expectancy to be fulfilled. These three stages describe a common sequence, but any one of them can occur without being accompanied by the others (see Figure 1.2).

Stage I. The first stage consists of learning information about the traits possessed by members of another group. When people are trying to learn about the traits possessed by others, they rely on one of two information-seeking strategies: They seek information most relevant to deciding whether the other person has the trait, or they seek information that confirms their preconceptions (Bodenhausen & Wyer, 1985; Devine, Hirt, & Gehrke, 1990; Duncan, 1976; Skov & Sherman, 1986; Sny-

Figure 1.2. Three-Stage Model of Stereotype Processing

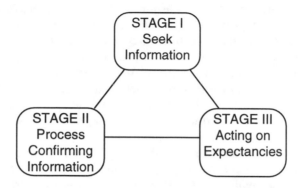

der & Swann, 1978; Trope & Bassok, 1983; Wilder & Allen, 1978). The tendency to engage in an unbiased search for information is likely to lead to sound judgments about the traits of others, but the tendency to seek expectancy-confirming evidence can lead to biased beliefs concerning the traits of others—beliefs that support stereotypes. One reason that people seek out expectancy-confirming evidence, rather than seeking out the best available information, is that confirming evidence is processed more easily (Skov & Sherman, 1986; Snyder, 1984). Also, in social interactions it is often more polite to ask questions of others that would tend to confirm preconceptions regarding their traits than to ask disconfirming questions (Dardenne & Leyens, 1995). That is, most people would be more comfortable asking a nun about her faith, rather than questioning her on her lack of faith. When people seek evidence that confirms their stereotypes, they apparently are unaware that they are gathering information in a biased manner.

A research example illustrates this process nicely. In this study college students were asked to test the hypothesis that their conversation partner was an introvert (Snyder & Swann, 1978). They were then given a list of questions that they could use during the interview. Many of the questions were designed to elicit information related to introversion (e.g., "What factors make it really hard for you to open up to other people?") and many were designed to elicit information related to extroversion (e.g., "In what kind of situations are you most talkative?"). Both types of questions could have provided information relevant to determining whether or not the other person was an introvert. The students were offered a reward of $25 if they could select the questions that would best test the hypothesis that the other person was an introvert. Despite the reward, the students mostly chose to ask questions that would elicit confirming rather than disconfirming information (i.e., questions that would bring out the other person's introverted side). Add to this bias a tendency to not even bother to gather information to test our ideas about stereotyped groups and we have another reason why stereotypes are so hard to change (Trope & Thompson, 1997). Thus, people may actively avoid information that disconfirms their stereotypes, although they may not be aware that they are doing so (Johnston, 1996).

> Confident expectation of a certain quality or intensity of impression will often make us sensibly see or hear it in an object which really falls far short of it. (James, 1890, p. 424)

Stage II. The second stage consists of the effects of expectancies on our perceptions of others. When stereotypes are activated, people pay more attention to expectancy-confirming information than to expectancy-disconfirming information (Bodenhausen & Wyer, 1985; Wyer & Martin, 1986). This confirming evidence then is stored and used as a basis for later judgments (Rothbart, Evans, & Fulero, 1979). When stereotypes have been activated, people often conclude that the behavior they have observed confirms their expectations, even when the behavior is ambiguous or does not confirm their expectations (Bodenhausen, 1988; Duncan, 1976; Major, Cozarelli, Testa, & McFarlin, 1988; Sagar & Schofield, 1980). In one study, White college students were shown videotapes of a disagreement that ended with one person giving the other what appeared to be a mild shove (Duncan, 1976). When the tape showed an African-American "shoving" a White person, 75% of the White students interpreted this as an act of violence, but when the tape showed a White person "shoving" an African-American, only 17% of the White students interpreted this as an act of violence. Like beauty, violence can be in the eye of the beholder.

These biases are not limited to race and ethnicity. For instance, it was found in another study that college students who viewed a videotape of a child's academic performance rated the child's ability at above grade level if they had been told beforehand that the child was from a high socioeconomic background. However, they rated her abilities as below grade level if they had been told she was from a low socioeconomic background (Darley & Gross, 1983). The students "saw" what their stereotypes led them to expect.

Not only do people pay more attention to evidence that confirms their expectations, they also tend to remember expectancy-confirming information better than expectancy-disconfirming information. Research indicates that expectancy-confirming information is best remembered when it concerns the traits, rather than the behaviors, of others, and when it concerns groups, rather than individuals (Stangor & McMillan, 1992). Thus, there appears to be a bias to remember trait information that is consistent with our stereotypes of groups (cf. Hamilton, Sherman, & Ruvolo, 1990).

Why is expectancy-confirming information better recalled than disconfirming information? Two factors have been identified. The first factor is that stereotype-disconfirming evidence often is discounted. Some "exceptions to the rule" are anticipated and these exceptions are not viewed as disconfirming the stereotype of the group as a whole (cf. Srull, Lichtenstein, & Rothbart, 1985; Stern, Marrs, Cole, & Millar, 1984). The second factor is that stereotype-based expectations often concern traits that are difficult to disconfirm (Hilton & von Hippel, 1990; Rothbart & John, 1985). As a result, even when disconfirming behavior occurs, it may not be recognized as such. For instance, consider this example from a study of desegregated middle schools (Schofield, 1980). Many of the White students in this study consider themselves to be unprejudiced and occasionally extend offers of help to African-American students.

> Black students often see such offers of help as just another example of White feelings of superiority and conceit. White students who do not perceive themselves as conceited feel mystified and angry when what to them seem to be friendly and helpful gestures are rejected. (p. 37)

In this case, the helpful behavior of Whites is not recognized as such by the African-American students, who instead see the behavior as confirming their stereotypes of Whites as conceited.

However, in certain circumstances disconfirming evidence is well remembered. People tend to remember disconfirming information when the trait expectancy is strong and the disconfirmation is clear (Srull et al., 1985). When expectancies are strong, it appears that disconfirming evidence is processed more thoroughly than confirming evidence (Hemsley & Marmurek, 1982; Srull et al., 1985; Stern et al., 1984). This thorough processing makes the disconfirming evidence easier to recall later. Thus, in order to change stereotypes it may be necessary to start by getting students to process stereotype-disconfirming information thoroughly.

To illustrate the second point, consider the traits of honesty and dishonesty. If you believe a person is honest, almost any dishonest behavior would be a clear disconfirmation of this trait, but if you believe a person is dishonest, honest behaviors are not necessarily seen as reflecting the underlying trait of honesty (the person may just be trying to make a good impression). This example suggests that it is harder to change a stereotype of dishonesty than one of honesty, and this may be true for other negative traits as well. Unfortunately, the stereotyped traits we most wish to change are usually negative (e.g., aggressive, arrogant, clannish, ignorant, lazy, loud, mean, unfriendly, untrustworthy), and people may disregard disconfirming evidence concerning such traits.

Even when disconfirming evidence is better remembered than confirming evidence, the impressions we have of the other person or the group may not change (e.g., Hastie & Kumar, 1979; Hemsley & Marmurek, 1982). The reason is that a stereotype will be weakened only if a trait is used to explain the disconfirming behavior (Crocker, Hannah, & Weber, 1983; Kulik, 1983). If the kind or generous behavior of a member of a group that is stereotyped as mean is explained in terms of the constraints of the situation (his mother asked him to help the elderly woman cross the street), then the behavior has been explained away and the stereotype will not change. Only if the kind behavior is explained in terms of some internal trait of the group member (his kindness) can the stereotype be altered. Thus, when stereotype-disconfirming evidence is explained in terms of situational constraints, the disconfirming evidence cannot contribute to stereotype change.

In general, people seem to be very conservative in allowing disconfirming information to influence their judgments of the traits of stereotyped groups (Grant & Holmes, 1981; Rasinski, Crocker, & Hastie, 1985). One technique that people use to avoid changing their stereotypes is that they subtype group members who behave in counterstereotypical ways (Hewstone, Hopkins, & Routh, 1992). For instance, African-Americans who excel in business may be subtyped as "high-achieving African-Americans," and the stereotypes of African-Americans in general will remain unchanged. When the behavior of members of stereotyped groups contradicts people's stereotypes, people appear quite willing to use almost any type of extraneous information to subtype these group members and avoid changing their stereotypes (Kunda & Oleson, 1995).

When people behave in ways that violate our stereotype-based expectancies, we tend to dislike or like them more than people whose behavior is consistent with pre-existing stereotypes (Bettencourt, Dill, Greathouse, Charlton, & Mulholland, 1997; Costrich, Feinstein, Kidder, Marachek, & Pascale, 1975; Deaux & Lewis, 1984; Jackson & Cash, 1985).

A member of a group that is expected to be very skilled in a given domain, but who performs poorly, may be more negatively evaluated than an individual who performs equally poorly, but was expected to perform poorly on the basis of his/her group membership. For instance, Whites may reject African-Americans who are not athletic or Asian-Americans who are not academically gifted simply because they violate the Whites' stereotypes of these groups. On the plus side of the ledger, African-Americans or Asian-Americans who violate negative stereotypes Whites hold of them by behaving in positive ways may be liked for doing so.

Taken together, the studies on expectancies reflect a powerful tendency to process information in ways that support pre-existing stereotypes, even when disconfirming information has been received (Wilder & Shapiro, 1991).

Stage III. The third stage of the expectancy–confirmation sequence concerns the relationship between expectancies and behavior. Expectancies frequently lead to self–fulfilling prophecies because people base their own behavior toward outgroup members on their stereotype-based expectancies (Fazio, Effrein, & Falender, 1981; Harris, Milich, Corbitt, Hoover, & Brady, 1992; Neuberg, 1996; Snyder, 1984; Snyder & Haugen, 1994; Snyder & Swann, 1978; Snyder, Tanke, & Berscheid, 1977; Word, Zanna, & Cooper, 1974). If teachers expect students from a given group to be slow learners (e.g., lower-class students), they may not assign difficult materials to these students and may give them less feedback and encouragement while working on these materials. The members of the group may react to being treated in this manner by acting in ways that confirm the initial low expectancies. For instance, the teachers' low expectancies may lead the students not to try very hard even on the relatively easy materials they have been assigned. Here is another example from Schofield's (1980) study of desegregated middle schools. In this school Whites had a stereotyped view of African-Americans as aggressive.

> Many [of the White students] are so afraid of Blacks that they do not stand up for themselves even in very nonthreatening encounters. This lack of willingness to assert themselves and to protect their own rights when interacting with Blacks makes Whites attractive targets [for aggression by Blacks] since their behavior also reinforces attempts to dominate them. (p. 40)

In this example the White students' expectations that African-Americans will behave aggressively toward them causes the Whites to behave timidly, leading African-Americans to respond with domination, thereby fulfilling the Whites' prophecies.

Some Additional Cognitive Biases That Influence Stereotyping

There is a bias in memory that leads people to recall that members of minority groups have engaged in negative behaviors more frequently than they actually have (Hamilton & Rose, 1980; Rothbart, Evans, & Fulero, 1979). When members of different groups come in contact, if the minority group members engage in stereotype-related negative behaviors, the majority group members may come away with exaggerated negative impressions. The tendency to overestimate the frequency of negative expected behaviors is enhanced when people are in a bad mood (Mackie et al., 1989). The tendency to overrecall negative, stereotype-confirming instances can be reduced by encouraging people to process the group and behavioral information in a conscious, thoughtful manner (Sanbonmatsu, Sherman, & Hamilton, 1987; Schaller & Maass, 1989).

Schaller (Schaller, Asp, Rosell, & Heim, 1996; Schaller & O'Brien, 1992) argues that stereotypes are due partly to faulty reasoning in everyday thought processes. When viewing the behavior of members of outgroups, people often explain it in terms of trait characteristics instead of situational factors. Many researchers argue that people have a powerful tendency to use traits to explain the behavior of others, especially negative behavior, and they make adjustments for potential situational causes only later, if at all (Gilbert, 1989; Jones & Nisbett, 1971). In intergroup contexts, students often fail to take situational factors into consideration when they should, resulting in stronger negative stereotypes of outgroups than the evidence warrants. Schaller and colleagues (1996) use as an example of this tendency the explanations people give for the fact that African-Americans score lower than Whites on national standardized achievement tests. Many Whites attribute these findings to a lack of intelligence on the part of African-Americans, failing to take into account such situational factors as biases in the tests, poor educational facilities, and a lack of exposure to relevant educational materials in their home environments. Whites frequently use similar blame-related explanations for crime and poverty. Schaller and his colleagues (1996) have found that briefly training college students in the logic of making statistically valid inferences reduces their tendency to form such erroneous group stereotypes.

The Relationship of Affect and Cognition in the Network Model

In this section the relationships between affect (feelings) and cognition (thoughts) in stereotype networks will be considered (cf. Bower, 1980; Clark & Isen, 1982; Fiske & Pavelchak, 1986, Fiske & Neuberg, 1989; Isen, 1982, 1984; Posner & Snyder, 1975; Stephan & Stephan, 1993). Affective reactions can be associated with all of the various types of cognitive nodes (group labels, traits, behaviors, exemplars) in stereotypes. The affect associated with group labels is of special interest. If the affect is predominantly negative and leads to a negative evaluation of the group, then the person may be said to be prejudiced toward that group. Obviously, affective reactions can vary in intensity. People have strong positive feelings about some groups and strong negative feelings (e.g., hatred, resentment, anger) about others. In addition, sometimes we have both positive and negative feelings toward the same group (Katz, Wackenhut, & Hass, 1986).

When a node for a social group becomes active, it activates the affective, as well as the cognitive, nodes to which it is linked (see Figure 1.3). For instance, when the node for "Hispanic" is activated, activation will spread not only to the trait nodes, but also to the nodes associated with feelings toward this group. In laboratory studies, one way that group nodes are activated is by briefly presenting the group label on a screen. Activating racial categories by presenting group labels has been found to influence the subsequent processing of stereotype-related traits. For instance, when the category "African-American" is activated by presenting the word "Black" to White students, the negative traits in the stereotype of African-Americans tend to be activated automatically (Dovidio, Evans, & Tyler, 1986). This activation then makes it possible for the students to quickly respond to questions about stereotype-related traits. For instance, they respond quickly by saying "yes" when asked if the word "lazy" can ever be used to describe African-Americans.

It appears that the activation of the group label automatically activates traits that are affectively consistent with the evaluation of the group (Neidenthal, 1990). If the group is liked, the traits that will be activated will be positive ones, but if the group is disliked, negative traits will be activated. Although the group label was presented as a written word to the students in the Dovidio studies, briefly presenting faces has a similar effect (Baker & Devine, 1988). The implications of

Figure 1.3. Affect and Cognition in Stereotypes

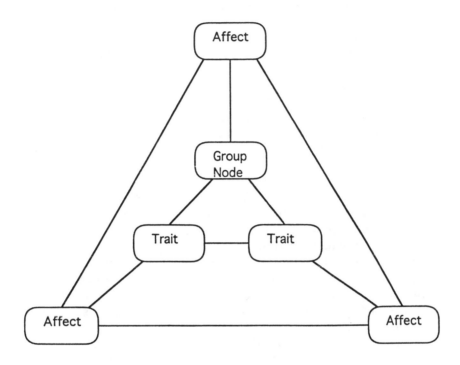

these findings are that during intergroup interaction, traits that are affectively consistent with the evaluation of the group will be activated automatically and will be readily available to be used as a basis for expectancies, attributions, behaviors, and subsequent judgments.

Moods also have been found to influence the processing of stereotype information. In general, when people are experiencing a positive affective state (i.e., a good mood) it facilitates the processing and retention of positive information (Bower, 1980; Mayer, 1989; Mayer & Salovey, 1988), although sometimes people in positive moods simply do not process information carefully (Mackie, Queller, Stroessner, & Hamilton, 1996). Likewise, negative affective states (particularly anxiety) typically facilitate the processing and retention of negative information. The differential processing of mood-congruent information can influence subsequent recall, evaluations, and other judgments (Erber, 1991; Mayer, 1989; Mayer, Gayle, Meehan, & Haarman, 1990). When people are experiencing positive or negative affect during intergroup interactions, they may process mood-congruent traits and behaviors more easily than mood-incongruent traits and behaviors. People in negative moods may pay attention to and recall the negative behaviors of others in ways that facilitate the creation and maintenance of negative stereotypes. People in negative moods also appear to be particularly prone to attribute negative traits to disliked outgroups (Esses, Haddock, & Zanna, 1993b).

Bodenhausen (1993) has argued that the effects of mood on stereotyping depend on two factors: (1) the ways in which a particular mood affects our ability to process information (processing capacity), and (2) the motivation to process information thoughtfully. Moods that produce high levels of arousal (e.g., fear, anger) reduce the capacity to process information thoughtfully. When moods cause this type of nonthoughtful processing, stereotypes tend to be relied on (Bodenhausen, Kramer, & Susser, 1993; Bodenhausen, Sheppard, & Kramer, 1994). We also rely on stereotypes when we are not motivated to pay careful attention to information that is available to us. Positive moods can undercut the motivation to process incoming information carefully, and when they do, it means that positive moods, too, can lead to a reliance on stereotypes (Mackie et al., 1996). On the other hand, if people in a positive mood are encouraged to process information carefully, the positive mood does not lead to a reliance on stereotyping (Mackie et al., 1996).

There is also a bias toward recalling information that is affectively consistent with attitudes toward social groups (Dutta, Kanungo, & Freibergs, 1972; Higgins & Rholes, 1978). One study found that when presented with equal amounts of positive and negative information about their ingroup and an outgroup, students subsequently recalled more of the positive than the negative traits that were attributed to the ingroup, while recalling more of the negative than the positive traits attributed to the outgroup. These memory biases tend to increase over time (Higgins & King, 1981). Thus, it appears that people have a tendency to remember the bad things that members of disliked groups do, while remembering the good things that members of liked groups do. Shakespeare had a similar idea in mind when he wrote, "The evil that men do lives after them; the good is oft interred with their bones" (Mark Antony in *Julius Caesar,* Act III, scene ii).

Before considering ways to counteract stereotypes, it may be useful to summarize what teachers are up against. The literature I have just reviewed indicates that stereotypes are frequently negative, overgeneralized, and incorrect. When we categorize others into social groups, we tend to exaggerate the differences between the groups and overemphasize the similarity of outgroup members to one another—*they* are all the same. We process information about outgroups in terms of traits, and this is especially true for negative information—we blame *them* for engaging in behaviors of which we disapprove. Stereotypes can be activated automatically, and when they are, the traits that are consistent with the person's feelings toward the group become the most accessible—for disliked groups, negative traits come to mind. When traits have been activated subconsciously, they often lead to more extreme judgments of members of other groups than are warranted by the evidence. When gathering information about the traits of others, we are prone to seek evidence that confirms our preconceptions and to disregard evidence that disconfirms our expectancies. We also tend to pay more attention to information confirming our stereotypes and we remember it better than disconfirming evidence. Our expectancies of others often serve as a basis for our behavior toward them, which can lead others to respond by confirming our expectations—the self-fulfilling prophecy. In addition, we tend to overestimate the frequency with which minority group members have engaged in negative behaviors. We are also susceptible to a bias that leads us to remember more negative than positive information about disliked groups. And when we are in a negative mood, it can lead us to focus on negative information about others. In the face of this formidable array of factors that support and sustain stereotypes, what can we do to change them?

CHANGING STEREOTYPES

Network models have a number of implications for stereotype change (cf. Crocker, Fiske, & Taylor, 1984). They tell us what needs to be changed and provide us with information on how to go about making these changes. In order to create more favorable stereotypes, links between group nodes and positive traits can be created or strengthened. Similarly, to reduce the impact of negative stereotypes, links between group nodes and negative traits can be weakened. It also may be possible to re-label negative traits with more desirable labels. In addition, new subtypes of the social category can be created or people can be encouraged to use superordinate categories that encompass both the ingroup and the outgroup within one category.

Strengthening or Creating Links to Positive Traits

Because the links between groups and traits are the basic elements of stereotypes, they will be our primary focus. Links between the group node and positive traits can be strengthened by the presentation of confirming instances. Creating positive moods in intergroup interactions may strengthen existing positive group/trait links because people may perceive such links to have occurred more frequently than they actually have (Mackie et al., 1989). Also, creating positive moods in intergroup interactions may increase the chances that information relevant to positive traits will be preferentially processed and remembered, while the processing of information relevant to negative traits may be inhibited. However, the research literature suggests that there is also the possibility that positive moods can reduce the motivation to process information thoughtfully and thus lead to a reliance on preexisting stereotypes.

New positive traits can be added to a stereotype by learning information about the group from others or through direct experiences with group members. To add new positive traits through direct experience, it is necessary for the trait-related behavior of group members to be attended to and processed and for trait explanations to be given for that behavior. The behavior is most likely to be attended to if it stands out in the situation (McArthur & Post, 1977; McArthur & Soloman, 1978). Trait attributions then must be made for the behavior. Trait explanations are most probable when group members consistently behave in distinctive ways that are not commonly displayed by members of other groups (cf. Kelley, 1967). For instance, if White students consistently behave in a friendly manner toward African-Americans in a variety of different contexts, African-Americans may come to explain these behaviors as being due to friendliness.

Although it may seem strange to try to change stereotypes by creating new stereotypes, this idea is based on the premise that stereotypes are ubiquitous and eliminating them may not be possible. In some instances, the most that can be hoped for is to change the favorability of the stereotype, rather than attempting to eliminate it. The stereotype may still be overgeneralized and possibly incorrect, but it may not be as harmful as the more negative stereotypes it replaces.

Weakening Links to Negative Traits

The process of weakening links between the group node and negative traits is more complex than strengthening positive group/trait links. Although it seems paradoxical, stereotypes may have to be activated through either automatic or conscious processing if the negative group/trait links are to be changed (Skowronski, Carlston, & Isham, 1993). If the group node is not activated, any disconfirming evidence that is presented cannot undo the group stereotype. For the example above, it would be necessary for the African-Americans to link friendliness to Whites by having the group node activated through either unconscious or conscious processes. That is, at some level the students would have to think about the person who is behaving in a friendly manner toward them as White for this information to change their stereotype of Whites as unfriendly. If the other person is not categorized as a group member ("Kathy is being friendly"), the stereotype of the group will not be altered.

For negative stereotypes to be modified, people must have sufficient cognitive resources available to process stereotype-related information (Gilbert & Hixon, 1991). That is, the situation should not place heavy mental processing demands on the individuals. The situation probably should not involve difficult tasks or create high levels of arousal, stress, or anxiety (Stephan & Stephan, 1985). If Hispanic students and African-American students interact with one another in a competitive setting (e.g., athletic contests between their schools), they are unlikely to change their stereotypes of one another, even if counterstereotypical behaviors occur, because competitive situations are often arousing, stressful, and anxiety provoking.

To weaken negative group/trait links the tendency in Stage I to seek out confirming evidence must be overcome. It appears that conscious, thoughtful processing of expectancy-related information can overcome the bias toward seeking confirming evidence. Another technique that has been found to be effective is leading students to consciously consider traits opposite to those that are expected (Lord, Lepper, & Preston, 1984). Also, if students are encouraged to seek evidence that disconfirms their expectations, they will do so (Snyder & White, 1981). In addition, it has been found that in situations in which ingroup members are dependent on outgroup members, increased effort goes into processing information about the outgroup (Borgida & Omoto, 1986; Erber & Fiske, 1984), thus increasing the chances that disconfirming evidence will be processed effectively (Darley, Fleming, Hilton, & Swann, 1986). Since dependence on outgroup members also could make ingroup members anxious or resentful, it might be best to create situations in which ingroup and outgroup members are interdependent, such as having students cooperate jointly to solve problems.

In Stage II, if disconfirming information is processed, it will not have an impact on eliminating the group/trait link unless the disconfirming evidence is explained in trait terms (Crocker et al., 1983). Rothbart and John (1985) have argued that disconfirming behavior is most likely to weaken stereotypes if it clearly disconfirms the stereotype and occurs frequently in a variety of settings. The processing of disconfirming evidence is further facilitated if the outgroup members who engage in the disconfirming behavior are perceived as otherwise typical (Rothbart & Lewis, 1988) and if the disconfirmations are strongly associated with the group label (Rothbart & John, 1985). Furthermore, the disconfirmations should be dispersed across a number of group members (Mackie, Allison, Worth, & Asuncion, 1992; Weber & Crocker, 1983). Under these rather stringent conditions, stereotype-disconfirming information about individual outgroup members should generalize to the group as a whole.

Other researchers have found that providing nonstereotype relevant information about individual group members, even when it is irrelevant to the stereotyped trait, can diminish the effects of stereotyping (Hilton & Fein, 1989; Locksley, Hepburn, & Ortiz, 1982). Apparently, the irrelevant information serves to remind people that they know little about the characteristics of the particular individual. One study showed that a completely meaningless bit of irrelevant individuating information (e.g., "the other person just got a haircut") reduced stereotype-related behavior on a task involving cooperation between a student and a member of the stereotyped group (deDreu, Yzerbyt, & Leyens, 1995). On the other hand, hearing about just one negative stereotype-confirming behavior of an outgroup member can increase the extent to which the group as a whole is stereotyped (Henderson-King & Nisbett, 1996). It appears to be relatively difficult to weaken negative stereotypes, but all too easy to strengthen them.

Other factors that lead to the thoughtful processing of disconfirming information also can facilitate the weakening of group/trait links. For instance, having students actively consider the response options open to the other person (Langer, Bashner, & Chanowitz, 1985), asking them to form accurate impressions (Neuberg, 1989, 1986, 1996; Srull et al., 1985; Stangor & McMillan, 1992), and creating low processing demands (Pratto & Bargh, 1991; Srull, 1981; Stangor & Duan, 1991) have been shown to promote the conscious, thoughtful processing of trait information. Furthermore, if the disconfirming evidence is positive in nature, it may be more likely to be processed and remembered by people who are in a positive mood.

In Stage III, changing stereotypes is inhibited by the tendency to create self-fulfilling prophecies. Fortunately, self-fulfilling prophecies are not inevitable. If the members of the stereotyped group are aware of others' negative expectations, they can counteract the expectancies successfully. They are particularly likely to counteract the expectancies if they are certain that they do not possess the expected trait (Swann & Ely, 1984). Also, students can be trained successfully to explicitly behave in disconfirming ways. In one study, African-American students were taught technical skills that enabled them to assemble a radio more quickly than their White counterparts, and this display of skill led to changes in the behavior of the White students toward the African-American students (Cohen & Roper, 1972). Thus, to change negative stereotypes it may be valuable for the people who are stereotyped to be aware of the associated expectations so they can counteract them. It also may be necessary to change their stereotypes of their own group, if they too subscribe to the negative stereotypes of their own group.

The effects of negative expectancies also can be offset when the students holding the stereotype try to get others to like them (Neuberg, 1996; Neuberg, Judice, Virdin, & Carillo, 1993). Therefore, when trying to change stereotypes through direct contact it may be useful to establish norms for the situation that encourage students to present themselves in likeable ways. For instance, students could be asked to engage in a dialogue with a student from another group and encouraged to try to create as positive an impression as possible.

Subtyping and Activating Alternative Categories

In addition to modifying the internal links within stereotype networks, it is also possible to reduce the use of stereotypes by adding new subtypes to a category or by substituting superordinate social categories. Breaking a category down into subtypes is promoted by the presentation of information that is inconsistent with current stereotypes and that is concentrated within a relatively small number of individuals (Weber & Crocker, 1983). Subtyping is also facilitated if disconfirming behavior occurs among group members who are not representative of the group in other ways (e.g., are atypical in terms of demographic characteristics) (Weber & Crocker, 1983). Subtyping may be particularly likely if members of a disliked group engage in disconfirming behavior that is unusually positive. They then may be grouped together as "exceptions to the rule" (Pettigrew, 1979a).

Although subtyping has the advantage of increasing category differentiation by creating subsets of outgroup members, it may not be beneficial if the subtypes that are created have stereotypes that are no more positive than the previously existing group stereotype. An additional problem is that creating subtypes still leaves the original stereotype unchanged and thus does not benefit people who continue to be categorized as members of the larger group. Further, the members of the sub-typed group are still likely to be treated as group members, rather than as individuals.

Substituting superordinate categories for categories lower in the hierarchy may be a more useful way of reducing the impact of stereotypes (Sherif, Harvey, White, Hood, & Sherif, 1961). When superordinate categories (e.g., the school, the community, the state, the nation, or the species) are evoked, outgroup members (e.g., African-Americans, Whites) become members of a more encompassing ingroup. In effect, this reappraisal converts entire outgroups into subtypes within the superordinate group. Cooperative interaction involving members of different subgroups has been shown to produce identification with the larger group and reduce intergroup bias (Gaertner, Mann, Dovidio, Murrell, & Pomare, 1990; Gaertner, Mann, Murrell, & Dovidio, 1989). In one study it was found that putting students in a pleasant mood also led to enhanced identification with a superordinate group and subsequently to less bias against a former outgroup (Dovidio, Gaertner, Isen, & Lowrance, 1995).

Altering Biased Labeling

When acknowledged differences between groups exist, the stereotype cannot be changed by eliminating the links between the category and the associated traits. In instances such as these, it may be possible to change the labeling of the trait from negative to positive. It is common for traits to be labeled negatively when they are applied to the outgroup, but for the same traits to be labeled positively if they are applied to the ingroup. The outgroup traits of fanatical, cunning, and pushy become devout, smart, and assertive when applied to the ingroup. Thus, positive labels often exist for stereotyped traits that are labeled negatively in the outgroup. Changing the labeling of group differences is one of the goals of the cultural sensitizer technique of improving intergroup relations (Brislin, Cushner, Cherrie, & Yong, 1986; Cushner & Landis, 1996; Triandis, 1976). This technique is designed to teach outgroup members to give the same explanations as ingroup members do for behaviors that are commonly perceived differently by the two groups (Weldon, Carlston, Rissman, Slobodin, & Triandis, 1975). Thus, a behavior that has been interpreted mistakenly as rejection, such as a Native-American not looking a member of another group in the eye, would be re-labeled as a sign of respect.

Mood and Stereotype Change

The results of studies of the effects of mood on attention, recall, evaluation, and judgment are complex. It appears that negative moods, especially those that detract from the ability or motivation to engage in conscious processing, have detrimental effects on intergroup perceptions. On the other hand, positive moods, especially those that do not detract from conscious information processing, may have beneficial effects on intergroup perceptions. Clearly, it is undesirable to have negative affect arise during intergroup interactions, particularly if it is caused by the outgroup. For instance, failure experiences, disagreements, anger, jealousy, fear, distress, and intergroup competition should be avoided when possible. On the other hand, positive affect, particularly if it is caused by the other group, should be fostered in intergroup contact situations. Thus, successful, enjoyable, or cooperative interactions should be encouraged whenever possible. An added benefit of creating positive affect during intergroup interaction is that it aids in linking positive affect to the outgroup, that is, it can reduce prejudice—the topic that we turn to next.

ADDITIONAL READINGS

Bar-Tal, D., Graumann, C. F., Kruglanski, A. W., & Stroebe, W. (Eds.). (1989). *Stereotypes and prejudice: Changing conceptions*. New York: Springer-Verlag.

Brewer, M. B., & Miller, N. (1996). *Intergroup relations*. Pacific Grove, CA: Brooks/Cole.

MaCrae, N. C., & Stangor, C. (1996). *Stereotypes and stereotyping*. New York: Guilford Press.

Oakes, P. J., Haslam, S. A., & Turner, J. C. (1994). *Stereotyping and social reality*. Cambridge, MA: Blackwell.

Chapter 2

PREJUDICE: THEORY AND RESEARCH

A group of eight Asian-American students are on a bus in Connecticut. The bus is taking this group, and a number of other students, to a formal dance. They are all dressed to the hilt. One of the Asian-American students feels something wet land in her hair. At first she thinks it is something that has dripped from the ceiling of the bus. Then she feels something warm and slimy hit her face and she realizes that it is spit. She turns to confront her attacker and is hit again with spit, this time in the eye. She screams, "Who did that?" and finds that a number of non-Asian students are spitting on the Asian students. Then they start calling the Asian students "chinks," "gooks," and "oriental faggots." A scuffle breaks out and the bus driver tells all the students to sit down and shut up, but the harassment continues until they arrive at the dance.

(adapted from Okihiro, 1993)

Prejudice can be defined as a negative attitude toward a social group (e.g., Newcomb, Turner, & Converse, 1965; Secord & Backman, 1964; Sherif & Sherif, 1956; Stephan, 1985). In addition to being negative, prejudicial attitudes are usually rigid, irrational, overgeneralized, and unjust (Ackerman & Jahoda, 1950; Allport, 1954; Kelman & Pettigrew, 1959; Simpson & Yinger, 1985). Although attitudes traditionally have been defined as including cognitions, affect, and behavioral predispositions (Secord & Backman, 1964), many recent definitions place the greatest emphasis on the evaluative or affective dimension of attitudes (Duckitt, 1992a, 1992b; Eagly & Chaiken, 1992; Esses, Haddock, & Zanna, 1993a; Olson & Zanna, 1993; Stephan, Ybarra, & Bachman, in press). In the case of prejudicial attitudes, this emphasis on evaluation makes good sense because it is the negative evaluation of outgroups that is the essential feature of prejudice. These negative evaluations merit out attention because they can have such negative consequences, as illustrated in the incident involving the Asian-American students.

Over the decades since the end of World War II, there has been a continuous decline in the willingness of White respondents in national surveys to admit that they are prejudiced. This decline in overt expressions of prejudice has sparked an interest in more subtle, covert manifestations of prejudice. A number of theories emerged during the 1970s and 1980s to explain the increasingly complex nature of prejudice. Although all of these theories initially were created to explain White prejudice toward African-Americans, all of them have now been applied to other types of prejudice, such as negative attitudes toward other ethnic groups, females, gays and lesbians, the disabled, and the elderly. Many of these theories trace their origins to the insights of Myrdal (1944) into the American character. Myrdal argued that there was a fundamental contradiction between White Americans' beliefs that all people are created equal and their willingness to use discrimination to maintain their dominant position. Most of the newer theories of prejudice embody some aspect of this two-sided dilemma—one side that fosters positive evaluations of outgroups and an opposing side that fosters negative evaluations of outgroups.

THEORIES OF PREJUDICE

Seven of these new theories of prejudice will be reviewed: symbolic racism theory, aversive racism theory, ambivalence-amplification theory, compunction theory, social dominance theory, social identity theory, and the integrated threat theory. Each theory discusses the nature of prejudice in its newer, often covert, forms and each addresses some of the causes and consequences of prejudice. The reason that I am covering so many of these theories is that each offers unique insights into the causes of prejudice and each has unique implications for techniques of reducing prejudice. The seven theories will be discussed first, followed by a brief discussion of the development of prejudice in children. The chapter concludes with a discussion of techniques for reducing prejudice.

Symbolic Racism Theory

Symbolic racism consists of a blend of anti-African-American feelings and a belief that African-Americans violate some of the traditional values embodied in the Protestant ethic, such as individualism, obedience, and self-reliance (Sears, 1988; Sears & Kinder, 1971, 1985). Symbolic racists are generally well educated and hold conservative political beliefs. They feel that African-Americans are pushing too hard for change and are moving too fast toward equality. They believe that racism is a thing of the past and that African-Americans do not deserve special treatment (e.g., affirmative action). Symbolic racism often is expressed as opposition to policies favoring African-Americans (Sears & Allen, 1984; Sears & Citrin, 1985) or voting against African-American political candidates (Sears & Kinder, 1971), but usually it is not expressed in overtly racist behavior (that is why it is called "symbolic" racism). According to this theory, Whites' opposition to a policy such as school desegregation is due not to the perception of threats to their own self-interests, but rather to the negative affect associated with African-Americans and the perception that African-Americans do not share the same values as Whites (Sears & Funk, 1991; Sears & Lau, 1983; Sears, Lau, Tyler, & Allen, 1980). A recent study makes the argument that a parallel type of symbolic sexism now characterizes men's relationships with women (Tougas, Brown, Beaton, & Joly, 1995). This study found that neosexism was related to men's opposition to affirmative action, as well as to more direct measures of negative attitudes toward women.

Aversive Racism Theory

Aversive racism theory (Dovidio & Gaertner, 1981; Gaertner & Dovidio, 1986) postulates that White Americans' racial attitudes are characterized by a contradiction between their values and their feelings. White Americans' beliefs in egalitarian values conflict with their unacknowledged negative feelings toward African-Americans (e.g., anxiety, discomfort, disdain). Aversive racists do not see themselves as racists, but they do feel anxious and uncomfortable in the presence of African-Americans and avoid them if they can do so conveniently. Aversive racists guard against overt discrimination against African-Americans in their own behavior, which enables them to maintain a self-image as being nonprejudiced. When an interracial situation is highly structured or clearly governed by social norms (e.g., a school board meeting), aversive racists typically stifle their negative feelings and act in egalitarian ways (Frey & Gaertner, 1986). If the nonprejudiced self-image of aversive racists is threatened, they may even act in excessively positive ways (Dovidio & Gaertner, 1983). For instance, if White students are worried that African-American students will think they are prejudiced, they may be excessively polite or helpful toward the African-Americans (which the latter may see as patronizing, thus actually making the problem worse). In contrast, in informal situations with conflicting or ambiguous social norms (e.g., an unsupervised playground), aversive racists may act in discriminatory ways (Dovidio & Gaertner, 1981; Gaertner & Dovidio, 1977).

Ambivalence-Amplification Theory

Ambivalence-amplification theorists believe that the attitudes that many people hold toward disadvantaged groups (e.g., minority groups, the poor, the disabled) are characterized by a deep ambivalence—a conflict between feelings of sympathy toward the plight of disadvantaged group members and an aversion to interacting with them (Katz, Glass, & Cohen, 1973; Katz, Glass, Lucido, & Farber, 1979; Katz, Wackenhut, & Hass, 1986). With respect to African-Americans, these theorists argue that Whites' beliefs in egalitarianism predispose them to feel sympathy for African-Americans and to support their struggle for equality. However, Whites' beliefs in individualism predispose them to be intolerant of African-Americans because the latter are perceived as deviating from the individualistic values of self-reliance, individual achievement, and motivation to work.

These ambivalent feelings lead Whites to experience tension when they interact with African-Americans. Aspects of the situation can amplify either the positive or negative side of these ambivalent attitudes, leading to amplified positive or negative behaviors toward African-Americans. When positive affect is salient, African-Americans are treated more favorably than Whites, but when negative affect is salient, Whites are treated more favorably than African-Americans (Katz et al., 1973; Katz et al., 1979). For example, when White and African-American students play together on the same team, the Whites may treat their African-American teammates very favorably as long as the team is winning, but their treatment of African-American teammates may turn quite negative if the team begins losing.

Compunction Theory

Compunction theorists believe that Whites growing up in our racially divided society learn the stereotypes of African-Americans at an early age (Devine, 1989; Devine, Monteith, Zuwerink, & Elliot, 1991). Whites are also exposed to the prejudices directed against African-Americans. Nonetheless, many White students come to believe that prejudice is wrong and they consciously hold nonprejudicial beliefs. However, the negative stereotypes of African-Americans still can be activated automatically by exposure to African-Americans, because these stereotypes were acquired so early during socialization that they reside deep within the mind of the individual. When these stereotypes are activated, low-prejudiced Whites intentionally inhibit the stereotype and attempt to act on their more recently acquired nonprejudiced beliefs. The activation of these old stereotypes or the failure to live up to their nonprejudicial standards can create feelings of guilt and self-criticism in low-prejudiced Whites. These feelings of guilt are labeled compunction in this theory.

The experience of compunction leads nonprejudiced students to learn how to regulate their behavior so that they can avoid behaving in discriminatory ways in the future (Monteith, 1993). This regulatory process occurs in four steps. When low-prejudiced students experience discrepancies between how they believe they should behave and how they actually have behaved, they (1) feel negative affect (guilt), which is directed toward the self; (2) focus on the self; (3) focus on the stimuli present when the discrepancy occurred; and (4) relate these stimuli to the discrepant response and feelings of guilt. Relating the guilt feelings to the situational context helps them to avoid behaving in prejudicial ways in similar situations in the future because the anticipation of guilt feelings will serve as a deterrent to prejudiced behavior. Thus, if students can be led to adopt nonprejudiced standards, this can set in motion a self-regulatory process that will reduce overt expressions of prejudice. Although high-prejudiced students also experience negative affect when they engage in discriminatory behavior, their negative affect (often in the form of anger) tends to be directed toward the other group, not the self (Monteith, Devine, & Zuwerink, 1993).

Social Dominance Theory

Social dominance theory argues that dominant groups in hierarchically structured societies adopt ideologies that serve to justify their status. These ideologies consist of legitimizing myths and symbolic attitudes that favor the existence of social inequality (Sidanius, 1993; Sidanius, Levin, & Pratto, 1996). For example, one widespread legitimizing myth consists of the belief that minority groups are innately inferior to the majority group. Their innate inferiority then is used by the majority group as a justification for discriminating against them. Within the majority group, the people who most strongly endorse group-based inequality tend to be the most prejudiced (Pratto, Sidanius, Stallworth, & Malle, 1994; Sidanius, 1993; Sidanius et al., 1996; Sidanius & Pratto, 1993.

According to social dominance theory, in racially stratified societies, such as the United States, prejudice and racism are means used by the majority group to maintain its position. Sexism works in a similar way; that is, people who favor social inequality also tend to be sexists (Pratto et al., 1994). The racism and sexism produced by this social dominance orientation ultimately lead to discrimination by high-power groups against low-power groups (Sidanius, 1993).

Social Identity Theory

Social identity consists of those aspects of self-identity that are based on group membership (Tajfel, 1978, 1982; Tajfel & Turner, 1979, 1986; Turner, Hogg, Oakes, Reicher, & Wetherell, 1987). The more strongly the ingroup members identify with their group, the more that outgroups will be perceived to be homogeneous and the stronger will be the tendency toward ingroup favoritism (i.e., evaluating and treating the ingroup more favorably than the outgroups). For example, Asian-American students who strongly identify with their ethnic group are likely to favor ingroup members over outgroup members and to see the members of outgroups as being alike. Making such favorable comparisons between the ingroup and the outgroup serves to enhance or maintain a positive self-image and thus provides a motivational basis for viewing outgroups negatively (Allen & Wilder, 1975; Billig & Tajfel, 1973; Haslam, Oakes, Turner, & McGarty, 1996; Tajfel, 1970). In fact, the motivation to maintain positive self-images is so powerful that merely categorizing people into groups can elicit ingroup favoritism (Billig & Tajfel, 1973; Tajfel, 1970; Turner, Brown, & Tajfel, 1979). Typically, the process of viewing the ingroup favorably involves comparing it with the outgroup on dimensions where it is possible for ingroup members to view their group as distinctively positive. For instance, Asian-Americans who are aware of the results of national standardized achievement tests, may view their group as more intelligent than other groups.

A recent extension of social identity theory discusses the role of authority figures, such as teachers, in creating a sense of pride and respect in group identities (Smith & Tyler, 1997). Tyler, Degoey, and Smith (1996) suggest that authority figures transmit two types of messages that can create pride and respect: (1) that the person is a valuable member of the group, which engenders self-respect, and (2) that the group as a whole is a worthy group, which can engender pride. The degree to which group members feel respect and pride in their group is tied to beliefs that the authority figures are trustworthy, fair, neutral, and respectful. The problem, as we will see, is to create pride and respect in the ingroup without causing rejection of outgroups.

Integrated Threat Theory

This theory integrates theories of prejudice that rely on one particularly important cause of prejudice—feelings of fear and threat. The idea

Figure 2.1. Model of Integrated Threat Theory

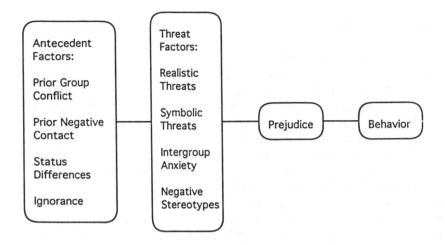

that fear and threat are at the root of prejudice runs through much of the intergroup relations literature, but only recently have attempts been made to conceptualize the various types of threats that may cause prejudice (Ashmore & Del Boca, 1976; Esses et al., 1993a; Greenberg, Pysczynski, Solomon, Rosenblatt, Veeder, Kirkland, & Lyon, 1990; Greenberg, Simon, Pysczynski, Solomon, & Chatel, 1992; Gudykunst, 1988; Sears, 1988; Stephan & Stephan, 1985, 1996b; Ybarra & Stephan, 1994). There appear to be four basic types of threats that lead to prejudice: realistic threats, symbolic threats, intergroup anxiety, and negative stereotypes (see Figure 2.1).

Realistic Threats. The realistic threats posed by the outgroup relate to the very existence of the ingroup (e.g., through open conflict), to the political and economic power of the ingroup, and to the physical or material well-being of the ingroup or its members (Ashmore & Del Boca, 1976; Bobo, 1988; Coser, 1956; LeVine & Campbell, 1972; Sherif, 1966). For instance, the battle of ethnic gangs for territory, prestige, and power results in the gangs posing real threats to one another. The theory emphasizes *subjectively* perceived threats posed by the other group (cf. Sherif, 1966) because the perception of threat can lead to prejudice, regardless of whether the threat is "real." The greater the threat the outgroup is perceived to pose to the ingroup, the more negative the attitudes toward the outgroup will be (Ashmore & Del Boca, 1976; Bovasso, 1993; LeVine & Campbell, 1972).

Symbolic Threats. Symbolic threats are founded in group differences in morals, values, norms, standards, beliefs, and attitudes. Symbolic threats are threats to the worldview of the ingroup. These threats arise because of a belief in the moral rightness of the ingroup's system of values. It is such beliefs that make groups ethnocentric, leading group members to believe their own group is superior to others (Sumner, 1906). Outgroups that hold values and beliefs that differ from those of the ingroup threaten the ingroup's value system, which leads to hostility toward the outgroups. For instance, one study found that when an ingroup's values, customs, or traditions were thought to be blocked by an outgroup, attitudes toward the outgroup were more negative (Esses et al., 1993a). The concepts of symbolic racism, social dominance, and ambivalence-amplification share much in common with the idea of symbolic threats. However, unlike these other concepts, symbolic threats can be experienced by minorities, disadvantaged groups, and subordinate groups, as well as by majority groups.

Intergroup Anxiety. People often feel personally threatened in intergroup interactions because they are concerned about negative outcomes, such as being embarrassed, rejected, ridiculed, or exploited (Stephan & Stephan, 1985). Anxiety is likely to be particularly high if the outgroup has a history of antagonism toward the ingroup, the group members have had little prior personal contact, and the ingroup knows little about the outgroup (Islam & Hewstone, 1993; Stephan & Stephan, 1985, 1989b, 1992). In addition to causing prejudice, intergroup anxiety also can cause avoidance of outgroups or lead to awkward behavior in the presence of outgroup members.

Consistent with compunction theory, even low-prejudiced members of the ingroup may be anxious when interacting with outgroup members because they fear that the negative stereotypes they hold might cause them to engage in behaviors that would be construed as prejudiced. Intergroup anxiety is similar to the unacknowledged negative affect that underlies aversive racism (Gaertner & Dovidio, 1986).

Negative Stereotypes. Although stereotypes are not usually thought of as threats posed by the outgroup, most outgroup stereotypes do embody threats to the ingroup because they contain negative traits. Negative traits generate negative expectations, and negative expectations lead ingroup members to fear that negative consequences will befall

them in the course of intergroup interaction. This fear of negative outcomes can create prejudice. If students think the members of an outgroup are mean, hostile, and aggressive, they are apt to dislike the
outgroup members. In fact, a number of studies have found that negative stereotypes are linked to prejudice (Eagly & Mladinic, 1989; Esses
et al., 1993a; Stangor, Sullivan, & Ford, 1991; Stephan, Ageyev, Coates-
Shrider, Stephan, & Abalakina, 1994; Stephan & Stephan, 1993).

Several factors can increase the experience of these four types of
threat in intergroup relations. Perceptions of threat appear to depend
on the level of prior conflict between the groups, the amount and type
of contact between the groups, the relative statuses of the groups, and
knowledge of the other group.

Prior Intergroup Conflict. Intergroup conflict is probably the single most
important seedbed of prejudice. The pivotal role that conflict plays in
causing prejudice is acknowledged in many theories of prejudice (Burton, 1986; Osgood, 1959; Patchen, 1988; Stephan & Stephan, 1996a). The
conflicts between groups that have occurred in the past serve as a
backdrop to current intergroup relations. Past conflict due to open con-
frontations, competition for scarce resources (e.g., elective positions,
money, territory, etc.), and disagreements over values and rights (e.g.,
religious values, cultural values, moral values) create feelings of threat
that can influence current relations.

Contact. The amount and type (positive or negative) of prior contact
between groups also affects feelings of threat. The greater the frequency of positive contacts (e.g., cooperative endeavors, successful
team efforts, pleasurable intergroup activities) relative to negative contacts (e.g., disagreements, fights, losing team efforts, unpleasant intergroup activities), the lower the threat, whereas the greater the frequency of negative to positive contact, the greater the threat. Thus,
students whose prior contacts with outgroup members have been predominantly negative are likely to feel threatened by the prospect of
future contacts with members of the outgroup.

Status. Perceived threats also may depend on the relative status or
power of the two groups. Both high- and low-status groups may feel
threatened by the other group, but probably for different reasons. Members of the high-status group may worry that the low-status group
would like to reverse the power relationships between them. They also
may be concerned about rejection, hostility, or resentment from the

lower-status group, or they may feel guilty about how their group has treated the low-status group.

Members of low-status groups may be concerned that high-status groups will dominate valuable resources, such as positions of power, or that they will use discrimination or force to maintain their domi- nance. Low-status groups are often afraid that high-status groups will try to impose their values on low-status groups. The low-status group members also may feel anxious when interacting with members of the dominant group.

Knowledge of the Outgroup. When ingroup members know very little about the outgroup, they are likely to perceive the outgroup as threat- ening. They will think that the other group is dissimilar to them and that its members probably dislike them. The fear here is a fear of the unknown, of the unfamiliar. The kind of knowledge that seems to be most useful in reducing this type of fear is knowledge of the subjective culture of the other group (Triandis, 1994). Thus, ingroup members are most likely to be fearful of the outgroup when they lack knowledge of the other group's beliefs, values, norms, roles, and behavior patterns. If fear is the father of prejudice, ignorance is its grandfather.

To summarize, when members of social groups have a history of conflict, have had limited positive contact or extensive negative con- tact, are discrepant in status, and know little of the other group, they are likely to feel threatened by the outgroup. These threats can take four forms, realistic threats, symbolic threats, intergroup anxiety, and negative stereotypes. The greater the perceived threats, the stronger the prejudice toward the outgroup. High levels of prejudice may be ac- companied by intense negative emotions such as anger, rage, resent- ment, and hatred, as well as hostile, aggressive, and discriminatory be- havior.

DEVELOPMENT OF INTERGROUP ATTITUDES

Prejudice does not just emerge, full blown, in adulthood. It gradually evolves through a process we are only now beginning to understand. The early developmental theories of racial attitudes argued that the cognitive and affective components of racial attitudes develop by some- what different mechanisms (Goodman, 1952; Katz, 1976; Rosenfield & Stephan, 1981). From ages 3 to 5 children learn to make distinctions between different groups, and by age 5 most children in America can categorize themselves and others correctly by race (Aboud & Doyle,

1993; Williams & Morland, 1976). By age 9 most children have acquired the stereotypes of African-Americans and Whites that are prevalent in our society (Brigham, 1974).

The developmental pattern for racial evaluations is quite different. White children show a strong preference for Whites as early as the preschool years (Williams & Morland, 1976). In the preschool years African-American children also prefer Whites (although not to the same degree as Whites do), but by the time African-American children have been in school for a year or two they come to prefer African-Americans.

One of the most fascinating aspects of the studies of racial classification and racial preferences is that "children's awareness of racial classification has little systematic relationship to [their preferences]" (Williams & Morland, 1976, p. 231). Apparently, this lack of relationship occurs because classification skills depend on the cognitive abilities involved in processing multidimensional information concerning the distinguishing features of social categories, whereas preferences are more closely related to socialization experiences involving how relations between groups are presented to children by their parents, siblings, teachers, peers, and the mass media (Rosenfield & Stephan, 1981).

More recent research suggests that there is a surprising change in children's racial attitudes after the age of about 7. Aboud and Doyle (1993) have demonstrated that children between the ages of 4 and 7 are highly ethnocentric, a result that is essentially in agreement with previous research. However, children between 7 and 10 years of age become less biased as they acquire more differentiated views of both the outgroup and the ingroup. By age 10 children display more balanced views of ethnic groups, views that contain both negative and positive elements for the ingroup and the outgroup. These findings have important implications for attempts to change prejudice. Attempts to alter attitudes and preferences that occur at a very early age (4–6) are likely to require different techniques and might not be as successful as those instituted at a somewhat older age (7–10) when children are developing more differentiated intergroup perceptions.

IMPLICATIONS OF THEORIES OF PREJUDICE FOR CHANGING PREJUDICE

The theories of prejudice I have just reviewed have very different implications for programs designed to reduce prejudice. The heart of the problem from the perspective of symbolic racism theorists is that African-Americans violate cherished values held by Whites, such as individualism, conformity to societal norms, and self-reliance. If it could be demonstrated to White students that most African-Americans and other minority groups do not violate their cherished values, their racism should be reduced. Symbolic racists think that discrimination is a thing of the past. If they could be convinced that discrimination is still very prevalent, one prop sustaining their views would be undercut.

From the perspective of aversive racism, one major problem is that Whites do not acknowledge that they harbor negative affect toward African-Americans. If Whites could be made more aware of this negative affect and if efforts then could be made to diminish these negative feelings, White students (those who would like to see themselves as nonprejudiced) would be less likely to avoid African-Americans and probably would behave more naturally around them. To overcome some of the potentially negative effects of aversive racism, intergroup contact should occur in relatively structured settings where there are clear norms against acting in prejudicial or discriminatory ways. Research indicates that if White students are confronted with the discrepancy between their beliefs in egalitarianism and their discriminatory behavior, they will change their behavior to be more in accord with their values (Rokeach, 1971).

From the perspective of ambivalence-amplification theory, the primary issue is to avoid activating negative emotions in intergroup contexts. Changing Whites' beliefs that African-Americans and other minority groups violate traditional values held by Whites, such as self-reliance, individual responsibility, and the value of hard work, could undercut the ambivalence that motivates negative response amplification. Strengthening beliefs in egalitarianism also should reduce ambivalence. One study indicates that beliefs in egalitarian/humanitarian values are consistently negatively correlated with both racism and sexism (Swim, Aiken, Hall, & Hunter, 1995).

Contact with outgroup members in situations with predominantly positive outcomes and a positive atmosphere also could erode the feelings of aversion that give rise to ambivalence. This suggestion is based on the most commonly used technique of treating phobias, known as systematic desensitization, in which fear is replaced with an emotion of opposite valence (usually relaxation). In an analogous fashion, negative feelings of aversion can be replaced with more positive feelings over time.

Compunction theorists would argue that students who are low in prejudice need to be reminded constantly of what actions may be construed as prejudiced or discriminatory, in order to set in motion the self-regulating processes that eliminate negative intergroup behaviors.

These theorists also might argue that intergroup contact should occur in settings where conscious, thoughtful information processing is fostered. If students who are not prejudiced are put in situations where they process intergroup information automatically, their stereotypes may have a negative impact on their behavior, even though they wish to behave in nonprejudicial ways. An even more challenging task is to start students who are currently high in prejudice on the road to becoming nonprejudiced and regulating their behavior. It appears that providing information on the societal disapproval of prejudicial behavior may not be the way to accomplish this goal, since this sometimes leads prejudiced students to direct even more prejudice toward the groups they dislike. It is not clear from this theory what would lead prejudiced students to reconsider their attitudes.

Social dominance theorists might argue that to reduce prejudice it is necessary to change the social system or at least to change the legitimizing beliefs that underpin the social dominance orientation (such as the belief that subordinate groups are innately inferior to the dominant group). The central issue here is that people who score high in social dominance orientation do not believe in equality between groups. Attempts to modify beliefs that justify inequality should reduce social dominance orientation and thereby reduce prejudice. If students could be convinced that group-based social inequality does not serve their own purposes or those of their group, social dominance orientations could be attenuated.

All five of these theories (symbolic racism, aversive racism, ambivalence-amplification, compunction theory, and social dominance theory) apply most forcefully to the prejudice of members of the majority group toward minority group members. Very little research has been done applying these theories to minority group prejudice toward the majority group, but each contains ideas that may generalize to minority group prejudice. The idea that prejudice will result when the other group is perceived to violate values cherished by the ingroup may apply as forcefully to minority group prejudice as to majority group prejudice. Feeling badly about behaving in ways that violate one's own values, which is a central feature in compunction theory, may be experienced by well-meaning minority group members as well as by members of the majority group. There is no reason to believe that minority group members are immune to justifying their relationships to other minority groups or even the majority group in ways that are just as self-serving as the legitimizing beliefs of the majority group (although the effects of minority group attitudes on the other groups are unlikely to be as negative as the legitimizing beliefs held by majority group members).

Social identity theory would appear to apply equally effectively to majority and minority groups. Social identity theorists would argue that intergroup interaction is more likely to reduce prejudice when it takes place at the interpersonal than at the intergroup level. Thus, from this perspective it would be important to de-emphasize group membership during intergroup interactions, perhaps by getting students to focus on others as individuals, not as group members. Anything that reduces the tendency to categorize others or the self at the group level should diminish prejudice in these settings. Creating interactions that do not threaten students' self-esteem also would help to eliminate bias in intergroup interactions.

It may be possible to undercut the tendency for the ingroup to disparage outgroups by reducing the need to build self-esteem through the use of positive comparisons to outgroups. When students are confident of themselves and their group identities, their motivation to disparage outgroups should be diminished. The motivation to disparage outgroups also may be reduced by encouraging students to view particular aspects of their own identities (e.g., race, ethnicity, religion) in the context of all of their other group identities (e.g., sex, age, school, community, state, nation). In addition, providing ingroup members with information about traits or skills where the outgroup is equal to or superior to the ingroup may counterbalance the tendency of the ingroup to make positive social comparisons to the outgroup on dimensions that favor the ingroup.

A major problem created by the tendency to disparage outgroups is that outgroup members are frequently on the receiving end of negative comparisons. A variety of strategies can be used to cope with these potentially damaging comparisons. For instance, outgroup members can seek out different dimensions on which they can make favorable comparisons to the group that is disparaging them. If dimensions favoring their own group are not readily available, the differences between the groups can be minimized or their importance can be diminished (Brewer, 1979). Another strategy to offset unfavorable comparisons is to choose different groups for comparison. For instance, minority group students might feel better when comparing their group with other minority groups (e.g., with respect to income) than when comparing themselves with the majority group.

The integrated threat theory also applies equally to majority and minority groups. Before initiating intergroup relations programs, administrators and teachers would do well to consider the factors that may be creating a climate of threat in their schools. Has there been a history of conflict between the racial and ethnic groups their students are

drawn from; how much positive or negative intergroup contact has occurred between the students themselves; are there large status differences between these groups in the community or school; and how
strongly are the students identified with their racial and ethnic groups?

The threat theory also may prove to be valuable in selecting techniques to be used in improving relations between the groups. For example, when symbolic threats are a primary cause of prejudice, stressing value similarities between the ingroup and the outgroup could allay
some of the fears of the ingroup members whose attitudes are most
negative. Students also could be helped to understand and respect the
group differences that do exist, instead of fearing them and negatively
evaluating them.

When perceived realistic threats are present in the school, it would
be helpful if group members could be led to see that some of these
perceived threats are unrealistic or overblown. It also might be possible
to reduce some realistic threats by making changes in school practices,
such as power sharing among groups.

It might be possible to reduce intergroup anxiety by training ingroup members in the "subjective culture" of the outgroup so they can
interact with outgroup members more effectively (Cushner & Landis,
1996; Triandis, 1972). Subjective culture refers to the implicit rules and
norms that guide social interaction among ingroup members. Outgroup
members are often ignorant of the subjective culture of the ingroup,
and this ignorance can lead to misperceptions and miscommunications.
When outgroup members are familiar with the subjective culture of the
ingroup, they can interact more effectively with members of the ingroup
and feel more comfortable in their presence. It also may be possible to
reduce anxiety in intergroup interaction by teaching students social
skills for interacting with mixed groups.

As mentioned in Chapter 1, negative stereotypes can be modified
through equal status contact with a variety of outgroup members who
behave in counterstereotypic ways in many different contexts (Rothbart & John, 1985; Stephan & Stephan, 1996a).

One important limitation of these theories is that they were all developed primarily to explain the prejudicial attitudes of college students or older adults. The degree to which they apply to children and
teenagers has not been well investigated. Unfortunately, the mechanisms by which children come to adopt more covert, rather than overt,
prejudicial attitudes is not known, nor is it known when children recognize that being overtly prejudiced may be considered inappropriate.
Similarly, we do not know when social identity issues begin to affect the
perceived differentiation of ingroup and outgroup members, or when

particular types of threats begin to become important causes of prejudice. The brief review of the development of racial attitudes that was presented earlier suggests that racial attitudes are more or less crystallized by ages 10 to 12, so it is likely that most of these theories can be applied usefully to middle school and senior high school students. These theories may not be as useful as a guide to understanding and changing the prejudices of younger students, particularly those below about age 7.

One task that educators face is deciding which of these theories applies to the situation that exists in their schools. To my knowledge, there are no assessment instruments to help in this analysis. It is clear that some of the theories are more oriented toward prejudice as it exists in the majority group (symbolic and aversive racism, ambivalence-amplification, compunction theory, and social dominance theory), and thus these approaches to prejudice are most likely to be useful in schools with predominantly majority group student bodies. Among these theories some may apply to students who come from more liberal backgrounds where prejudice and stereotyping are considered to be wrong (e.g., compunction theory, ambivalence-amplification theory), others would seem to apply to students starting from a very early age (e.g., aversive racism), and some seem specifically targeted at students influenced by the Protestant ethic (e.g., symbolic racism). Two theories, social identity theory and integrated threat theory, would appear to be useful in diagnosing problems in multiethnic schools, particularly those with predominantly minority group student bodies. In any school context, I think it is important to try to understand the nature of the prejudices that exist in the school, and their causes, so that this information can be used as a basis for selecting techniques of improving intergroup relations (these will be covered in Chapter 4).

To this point, I have reviewed basic theories and research on stereotyping and prejudice. In the next chapter I will examine the conditions under which stereotyping and prejudice come into play. The primary focus will be on the circumstances in which intergroup contact has the most beneficial effects on stereotyping and prejudice.

ADDITIONAL READINGS

Aboud, F. E. (1988). *Children and prejudice*. Cambridge, MA: Blackwell.
Brown, R. (1995). *Prejudice*. Cambridge, MA: Blackwell.
Jones, J. M. (1997). *Prejudice and racism* (2nd ed.). New York: McGraw-Hill.

Chapter 3

CONTACT THEORY

Prejudice (unless deeply rooted in the character structure of the individual) may be reduced by equal status contact between majority and minority groups in the pursuit of common goals. The effect is greatly enhanced if this contact is sanctioned by institutional supports (i.e., by law, custom or local atmosphere), and if it is of the sort that leads to the perception of common interests and common humanity between the members of the two groups.

—Allport, 1954, p. 267

The contact hypothesis was formulated after World War II ended. American social scientists were full of optimism after winning the war. They returned home ready and willing to confront America's domestic ills. They believed that the age-old social problems of poverty, crime, and prejudice could be eliminated once and for all. One of the solutions they proposed to address prejudice came to be known as the contact hypothesis. The social scientists who developed the various versions of the contact hypothesis were fully aware of the complexity of the issues involved (Pettigrew, 1986). The quote from Gordon Allport cited above illustrates the fact that they did not think eliminating prejudice was a simple matter that could be accomplished merely by bringing people from different groups together, and they did not think it could be accomplished quickly. They were right on both counts. But their insights into intergroup contact had a profound impact on the way that people came to think about relations between groups. Their ideas encouraged other social scientists to start thinking about and testing techniques that could be used to foster the optimal contact conditions. As we shall see, even today the contact hypothesis is still the basis of many of the most widely used techniques of improving intergroup relations.

In this chapter I will review the research that has been done on intergroup contact. The chapter has two sections. The first section consists of a discussion of factors that increase the chances that intergroup contact will lead to improvements in intergroup relations. The second section examines the effects of school desegregation on intergroup relations.

CONTACT HYPOTHESIS

The initial versions of the contact hypothesis focused primarily on the effects of factors within the contact situation that affect prejudice (Allport et al., 1953; Allport, 1954; Harding, Kutner, Proshansky, & Chein, 1954; Watson, 1947; Williams, 1947). This focus on situational factors led researchers to be interested primarily in variables that could be controlled in actual intergroup encounters. These researchers were less interested in the structural factors that cause prejudice than in changes that could be made in situational factors that would improve intergroup relations. Four factors were central to the early formulations of the contact hypothesis (Stephan & Stephan, 1996a).

- Cooperative interaction
- Equal status among the participants
- Individualized contact
- Institutional support for the contact

The early contact theorists believed that if people could be brought together in school, work, recreational, or other settings under these conditions, improvements in intergroup relations would ensue. I will review briefly the evidence on each of these four factors.

Cooperation

No factor associated with intergroup contact has received more attention than cooperation (Johnson & Johnson, 1992a; Johnson, Johnson, & Maruyama, 1984; Miller & Harrington, 1992; Slavin, 1985, 1992; Worchel, 1986). Hundreds of studies provide strong support for the proposition that when people cooperate together in mixed groups, intergroup relations improve. This research suggests that cooperation is most effective when it leads to successful outcomes (Blanchard, Adelman, & Cook, 1975), measures are taken to avoid the negative effects of different levels of task ability (Cohen, 1980, 1984; Slavin, 1978), the ingroup and the outgroup are similar in attitudes (Brown & Abrams, 1986), and assignment to groups does not make social categories salient (Miller,

Brewer, & Edwards, 1985; Miller & Harrington, 1990). In small group settings, balanced ratios of ingroup and outgroup members have been found to be most beneficial (Gonzales, 1979; Miller & Davidson-Pod-gorny, 1987). However, in large group settings, balanced ratios may threaten the majority group and can have negative effects on intergroup relations (Hallinan & Smith, 1985; Hoffman, 1985; Longshore, 1982).

Even under the best of conditions, the changes in attitudes toward individual outgroup members brought about by cooperation may not generalize to the outgroup as a whole (Blaney, Stephan, Rosenfield, Aronson, & Sikes 1977; Brewer & Miller, 1988; Longshore, 1982; Weigel, Wiser, & Cook, 1975). Structuring intergroup cooperative learning tasks so that they produce positive interactions with outgroup members can facilitate generalization to the group as a whole (Desforges et al., 1991). That is, it appears to be important that the interactions be engaging, enjoyable, rewarding, and successful. It also appears that encouraging the members of cooperative groups to maintain an interpersonal focus during their interactions leads to a generalization of positive behavior toward outgroup members, while encouraging a task focus does not (Rogers, 1982, cited in Brewer & Miller, 1988; see also Miller & Harrington, 1990).

The effects of working together in mixed cooperative groups are not diminished, and may even be enhanced, by *inter-team* competition (Slavin, 1985, 1990, 1992). The beneficial effects of inter-team competition are most likely to appear in situations in which the outcomes are successful. When mixed groups fail, there is a danger that the outgroup members within the mixed groups will be blamed for the failure (Blanchard, Adelman, & Cook, 1975; Burnstein & McCrae, 1962; Rosenfield, Stephan, & Lucker, 1981). Another limitation of competition is that it increases motivation primarily for individuals with high achievement levels (Epstein & Harackiewicz, 1992).

Equal Status

There are two types of equal status that must be taken into consideration in contact situations: equal status on demographic factors external to the contact situation (socioeconomic status, age, education), and equal status within the contact situation (Cohen & Roper, 1972; Norvel & Worchel, 1981; Pettigrew, 1969; Riordan, 1978). Equal status on factors external to the contact situation is difficult to achieve in societies like ours that are stratified by racial, ethnic, and social class hierarchies (Riordan, 1978). When equal status on external factors does occur, it has positive effects on intergroup perceptions, apparently because equal status increases the chances that similarities between individuals from different groups will be noticed (McClendon, 1974). For instance, one study found that White students had favorable attitudes toward African-Americans if they had friendships with minority group members who were of equal or higher social status than themselves. Friendships with lower-status African-Americans produced attitudes that were no more favorable than no contact at all (Jackman & Crane, 1986).

Due to the differences in socioeconomic status between African-Americans and Whites, the majority of contacts White students have with African-Americans are likely to be with lower-status African-Americans, and this may account for the fact that even positive contacts between African-Americans and Whites often do not change Whites' attitudes.

When equal status on factors external to the situation cannot be arranged, it appears that creating equal status roles within the contact setting can still improve intergroup relations. Cooperation between students from different groups who have equal status in the contact setting can have positive effects on intergroup perceptions, even when the students differ in status on factors external to the situation (Aronson, Blaney, Stephan, Sikes, & Snapp, 1978; Weigel, Wiser, & Cook, 1975).

The ideal arrangement for intergroup contacts would be to have equal status both on demographic factors external to the situation and on relevant dimensions (e.g., role assignments) within the situation. If equal status on external factors cannot be arranged, at least there should be an attempt to arrange for equal status within the contact situation. When status inequalities do occur, it would appear to be better for the minority group members to have higher status than the majority group members (cf. Cohen, 1980), if this is possible.

Individualized Contact

Traditional contact theory suggests that intergroup contact should be nonsuperficial and offer students the opportunity to get to know one another as individuals (Amir, 1976). A number of studies indicate that providing students with information about the behavior of individual group members can influence perceptions of those individuals and that their social categories are de-emphasized in this process (Locksley, Borgida, Brekke, & Hepburn, 1980; Locksley et al., 1982). However, information about the behavior of individual outgroup members may not have these potentially beneficial effects if the positive behaviors are not displayed consistently or if strong stereotypes are associated with the social group to which the individuals belong (Grant & Holmes, 1981; Krueger & Rothbart, 1988). When strong stereotypes exist, the behavior of an individual who disconfirms the stereotype may be noted, but it may be explained away by attributing it to factors in the situation.

When creating small group contact opportunities in school, work, or other settings, an interesting and complex problem must be confronted. Should the interactions that occur take place at the *interpersonal* or the *intergroup* level (Hewstone & Brown, 1986). Interpersonal interaction occurs when the participants are encouraged to treat one another as individuals, rather than as members of distinct social groups. Intergroup interaction is the reverse: Participants see one another as group members, rather than as individuals.

Miller and Brewer favor an emphasis on interpersonal interaction among individual group members (Brewer & Miller, 1984, 1988; Miller & Harrington, 1990, 1992). They argue that only when group factors are de-emphasized, are members of outgroups likely to be differentiated and treated as individuals. According to Brewer and Miller (1984), "Differentiated and personalized interactions are necessary before intergroup contact can lead to group acceptance and reduction of social competition" (p. 288). In support of their position, several studies have found that assignment to small cooperative work groups on the basis of criteria unrelated to social categories (such as seating positions in a classroom) produces more favorable treatment of members of other groups than assignment according to category membership (Bettencourt, Brewer, Rogers-Croak, & Miller, 1992; Miller et al., 1985; Miller & Harrington, 1990). Thus, creating the conditions under which individualized contact was likely to occur promoted favorable intergroup relations in these studies.

In contrast, Hewstone and Brown (1986) argue that treating outgroup members as individuals, rather than as group members, is not likely to lead to changes in attitudes toward the group as a whole. The problem is that, by placing social groups in the background, interpersonal interactions are less likely to change intergroup relations because the individual outgroup members will not be viewed as members of social groups. In addition, it may be difficult to modify stereotypes unless social groups are made salient so that disconfirmations of category-based expectancies will be noted (Rothbart & John, 1985). Hewstone and Brown argue that group identities should be made salient during intergroup contact in order to maximize the possibilities that any positive changes that are brought about by the contact situation will generalize to the outgroup as a whole (Vivian, Hewstone, & Brown, 1994). Many teachers feel that they should try to act as if the ethnic identities of their students were invisible, but Hewstone and Brown probably would argue that it may be better to respectfully acknowledge the existence of the diverse ethnic backgrounds of their students. Additional research is required to determine the conditions under which each type of interaction (interpersonal and intergroup) is most effective. It is possible that de-emphasizing group membership may be more effective in reducing prejudice than in changing stereotypes, whereas making group membership salient may be more effective in changing stereotypes than in reducing prejudice. One solution to this dilemma would be to assign students to mixed groups on some basis other than race or ethnicity (e.g., last name, having them count off by number), but then not to discourage the use of racial or ethnic categories during the group interactions (unless the students use the categories in disparaging ways).

Support by Authorities

Support by respected authority figures, such as administrators, teachers, school board members, and parents, appears to enhance the effects of intergroup contact (Adlerfer, 1982; Aronson et al., 1978; Cohen, 1980; Slavin, 1985; Williams, 1977). However, there are limiting conditions to these beneficial effects. Cohen (1980) has argued that it may be difficult to create equal-status interactions between groups of students when the administrators and teachers are not drawn from all of the groups represented among the students. Also, it may be difficult to improve intergroup relations when the contact is imposed by authorities, because students sometimes react negatively to a loss of control over their freedom of association.

It is clear that positive intergroup relations can occur in the absence of explicit support by authority figures, as often happens in intergroup friendships (Blumberg & Roye, 1980). Studies that have examined voluntary informal contact typically find that such contact leads to favorable outgroup attitudes (Carter, DeTine, Spero, & Benson, 1975; Masson & Verkuyten, 1993; Stephan & Rosenfield, 1978b; Stephan & Stephan, 1984; Webster, 1961). The greatest improvements in intergroup relations are likely when ingroup and outgroup authority figures promote voluntary intergroup relationships.

Administrators and teachers in the schools are responsible for setting the tone for intergroup relations in their schools. Blanchard (1992) has suggested that administrators should establish two types of policies concerning intergroup relations. The first type of policy is directed at the well-intentioned majority of students who realize that expressing

prejudice and acting on negative stereotypes is wrong, but who occasionally make mistakes and act in callous or discriminatory ways (often
through ignorance or lack of experience in intergroup relations). For
these students, norms of civility, tolerance, and respect should be promoted through the creation of school policies that openly approve of
such behaviors. These policies could be created by administrators and
teachers, but they also could be generated through consensus among
the students, perhaps through their governing bodies. They also can
be promoted in intergroup relations programs.

For the small number of students who are prejudiced and hostile,
strong codes of conduct should be established that punish intentional
hate speech and acts of intergroup aggression. As Schofield (1995) suggests, "Children [should] know that they cannot violate others' rights
with impunity" (p. 276).

UPDATED CONTACT THEORY

In addition to the basic four factors included in the original statements
of the contact hypothesis, a number of other factors relevant to the
success of intergroup contact situations have been investigated. These
factors can be divided into two different types: societal and person.

Societal Factors

Cook (1962) suggested that if members of the participants' ingroup
have favorable norms and attitudes toward intergroup contact, the participants should be made aware of this fact. Consistent with Cook's suggestion, Secord and Backman (1964) argued that positive intergroup
relations tend to prevail when the central values of the society favor
intergroup contact (see also Williams, 1964). Other societal variables
that have been investigated include the prior relations between the par-
ticipating groups (Brislin & Pedersen, 1976; Tajfel, 1981; Williams, 1977)
and the degree of acculturation of minority groups (Eshel & Peres,
1973). Intergroup contact is more likely to improve intergroup relations
if prior relations between the groups have not been antagonistic and if
the minority groups are acculturated. Schofield (1991) has called for
greater attention to problems created by cultural differences among the
groups that come together in contact situations. For instance, Mexican-
American students have been reported to be more deferential to authority than students from many other ethnic groups, and they tend to
be less competitive (Kagan, 1980; Phinney & Rotheram, 1987). Thus, in

Figure 3.1. Causal Model of the Contact Hypothesis

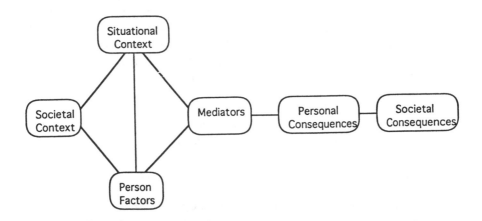

addition to factors within the contact situation, researchers have begun
to pay more attention to the broader social context in which intergroup
contact occurs.

Person Factors

Considerable research has been done on the characteristics of the participants in intergroup contact. These person factors include demographic variables (positive changes are considered most likely with
younger, better educated, higher social class individuals) (Williams,
1964), personality traits such as self-esteem and authoritarianism (Stephan & Rosenfield, 1978b; Wagner & Schonbach, 1984; Weigel & Howes,
1985), and competence in task-relevant skills (Blanchard & Cook, 1976;
Cohen & Roper, 1972; Rosenfield et al., 1981). Although these factors
are usually not under teachers' control, they do suggest that contact
programs are likely to be more successful with some student populations than with others.

   More than a decade ago, I attempted to create a theoretical model
based on the research that has been done on the contact hypothesis
(Stephan, 1987). The theoretical model I created can be seen in Figure
3.1. This model indicates that societal factors influence situation and
person factors. The situation and person factors influence one another.
The model explicitly notes that there are factors that mediate the effects of the person and situation variables on subsequent behavior, cog-

nitions, and affect. Finally, the model indicates that changes in individu-als ultimately can bring about changes in society (Bochner, 1982).

Among the categories of *societal context* variables that appear to be important are: (1) the structure of the society, especially its stratifi-cation system (the emphasis a society places on distinctions of socio-economic status, age, gender, religion, race and ethnicity, etc.), (2) the historical relations between the groups that are in contact with one another, (3) the current relations between these groups, and (4) the cultural backgrounds of the groups.

The variables that constitute the *situational context* in which the contact takes place can be categorized as follows: (1) the setting in which the contact occurs, (2) the nature of the interaction, (3) the com-position of the groups, and (4) the task in which the participants are in-volved.

The *person factors* comprise: (1) demographic characteristics, (2) personality traits, and (3) prejudices, stereotypes, and other beliefs.

The proposed *mediators* of the effects of contact are: (1) behavioral, (2) cognitive, and (3) affective processes.

The principal *personal consequences* include: (1) behaviors, (2) cog-nitions (particularly stereotypes), and (3) evaluative reactions (particu-larly prejudice).

The *societal consequences* concern the effects of contact on future relations between groups. These changes could include modifications in public attitudes (especially prejudice and stereotypes), alterations in social norms or the legal system (e.g., laws against discrimination), and modifications in the relative economic or political status of the groups.

The model has implications for contact in school settings as well as for empirical research. Empirically, the model makes explicit the in-terrelationships among these factors and specifies the causal relation-ships between the factors. For instance, it implies that societal factors shape the kinds of situations in which contact takes place, but it also implies that the contact that takes place in those situations may change relations between the groups in society and therefore affect future con-tact situations. The model further suggests an array of variables within each category that may have an impact in any intergroup contact situa-tion (see Table 3.1).

From an applied perspective, the model indicates the domains of factors that should be considered in attempts to improve intergroup relations in the schools. For example, in designing an intergroup rela-tions program involving intergroup contact, the model suggests that teachers should start by considering the societal context in which the

Table 3.1. Variables Relevant to the Contact Model

Societal Context	Situational Context	Person Factors
Social Structure	Setting	Demographic Characteristics
Social Stratification	Physical Setting	Personality Traits
Historical Relations	Seating Patterns	Task and Social Abilities
Prior Contact	Nature of Interaction	Cognitions
Degree of Conflict	Goals	Beliefs
Current Relations	Structured/Unstructured	Stereotypes
Amount of Contact	Superficial/Intimate	Prejudice
Quality of Contact	Formal/Informal	Ethnocentrism
Degree of Conflict	Positive/Negative	Expectancies
Cultural Background	Authority Support	Values
Socialization Practices	Equal/Unequal Status	Affect
Subjective Culture	Equal/Unequal Power	Threat Feelings
Social Norms and Roles	Cooperative/Competitive	
	Short/Long Term	
	Task	
	Interpersonal/Task Oriented	
	Success/Failure	
	Administration/Faculty/Staff	
	Racial/Ethnic Composition	

Mediators	Person Consequences	Societal Consequences
Behavioral	Behavior	Changes in Public Opinion
Modeling	Positive/Negative	Changes in Public Policy
Rewards/Punishment	Short/Long Term	Changes in Discrimination
Cognitive	Cognitive	Changes in the Distribution
Attention	Stereotypes	of Political Power
Encoding	Prejudice	Changes in Minority
Storage	Expectancies	Educational Achievement
Retrieval	Ethnocentrism	Changes in Ethnic
Affective	Affective	Distributions Across
Classical Conditioning	Positive/Negative	Occupations

contact is taking place. What is the nature of the stratification system; how have the groups related to one another in the past; what social norms exist concerning intergroup contact; what socialization practices differ between groups (e.g., respect for authority) that may affect how the groups interact with one another and teachers; and what are the cultural backgrounds of the students? Teachers obviously must pay special attention to situational factors such as the setting, the nature of the interaction (cooperative, voluntary, etc.), the composition of the groups (ingroup/outgroup ratio, relative statuses), the type of relationships that will be fostered (interpersonal or intergroup), and the type of task to be performed. In addition, person factors such as personality traits (authoritarianism, self-esteem), demographic characteristics (socioeconomic status, gender, religion), stereotypes, and levels of prejudice should be taken into consideration. Some thought also should be devoted to maximizing the mediators of changes in prejudice and stereotypes, including such things as rewards for appropriate conduct and punishments for inappropriate conduct, modeling of appropriate conduct, creating an optimal information processing environment (e.g., minimizing stress and anxiety and avoiding high processing demands that interfere with thoughtful processing), and creating positive affect. Finally, careful consideration should be given to the goals of the program—is it designed to change stereotypes (which ones), prejudice, or discriminatory behavior (which specific types)?

At about the same time that the contact hypothesis was formulated, the first court cases that ultimately would lead to the *Brown* v. *Board of Education* (1954) decision on school desegregation were filed. School desegregation was like a large-scale experiment in intergroup contact. In the next section I will use my model of the contact hypothesis to help explain what the effects of desegregation have been and why they occurred.

SCHOOL DESEGREGATION

Does segregation of children in the public schools solely on the basis of race, even though the physical facilities and other "tangible" factors be equal, deprive the children of the minority group of equal educational opportunities? We believe that it does. . . . To separate Negro school children from others of similar age and qualifications solely because of their race generates a feeling of inferiority as to their status in the community that may affect their hearts and minds in a way unlikely ever to be undone. . . . We conclude that in the field of public education the doctrine of "separate but equal" has no place. Separate educational facilities are inherently unequal. (*Brown* v. *Board of Education,* 1954)

One of the goals of school desegregation was to improve intergroup relations (Stephan, 1978, 1986, 1991; Stephan & Stephan, 1996a). Thus, it is reasonable to ask what the effects of school desegregation on intergroup relations have been. Before addressing this question, it may be useful to put desegregation in historical perspective.

For the decade following the 1954 Supreme Court decision in

Brown, desegregation moved very slowly. However, with the passage of the 1964 Civil Rights Bill, desegregation began to take place at a more rapid rate. Nearly all of the desegregation that has occurred in the United States took place during the decade between 1964 and 1974. By 1972, 44% of African-American children in the South were attending schools in which the majority of students were White, while in the North 29% of African-American children were attending such schools (Pettigrew, 1975). By 1980, 70% of African-American students were attending school with some Whites (more than 5% White). However, a similar percentage of Whites (69%) attended schools that were *less* than 5% African-American (U.S. Commission on Civil Rights, 1987). As in the 1970s, the South was more integrated than the North, with the West falling in between. The most recent evidence indicates a trend toward resegregation of American schools (Orfield & Eaton, 1996). This resegregation has occurred because the inner cities of America's urban areas are becoming increasing segregated, there have been substantial increases in the size of minority populations due to their birth rates and immigration, segregation in housing is widespread, and a number of desegregation plans have been allowed to lapse or have been modified by court orders.

Short-Term Effects

Did desegregation lead to decreases in prejudice? A review of the empirical studies indicates that for African-Americans desegregation reduced prejudice toward Whites in more cases than it increased prejudice (38% vs. 24%) (Stephan, 1986, 1991). However, for Whites, the results were just the opposite. Desegregation increased prejudice toward African-Americans in more cases (48%) than it decreased it (16%). These studies suggest that, in the short run, desegregation did not produce the positive effects on prejudice that had been anticipated.

However, a note of caution should be sounded concerning these studies of the short-term effects of desegregation on prejudice. Comparing these studies with one another is often difficult because they were conducted in different regions of the country, the types of desegregation plans that were examined varied from study to study, the age of the students differed across studies, the racial composition of the communities was rarely the same, and the amount of opposition to desegregation in these communities varied considerably. Also, these studies dealt primarily with the experiences of African-American and White schoolchildren during the first year or so of desegregation. The initial year of desegregation is a very unusual experience for most students.

Not only are they attending newly desegregated schools, but desegregation often is accompanied by community opposition, anxiety on the part of students and parents, and changes in curriculum and teaching staffs.

As the mixed results concerning the short-term effects of desegregation began to emerge in the 1970s and 1980s, controversy arose over why desegregation was not more successful (Cook, 1979, 1984; Gerard, 1983). Cook (1979) used the contact hypothesis to explain why school desegregation did not have more positive effects on intergroup relations in the short term. In Cook's view, desegregation did not have more positive effects because the conditions set forth in the original versions of the contact hypothesis rarely existed in desegregated schools. Desegregation often was introduced by reluctant authorities, in schools where competition was characteristic, where cliques, tracking, and other factors that foster within-school segregation prevented individualized contact, and where equal-status contact between African-Americans and Whites was the exception, rather than the rule (Schofield, 1991).

Long-Term Effects

Until the 1980s it was impossible to study the long-term effects of desegregation because there were so few students who had graduated from desegregated schools. However, a number of studies have now been completed that examine the effects of attending desegregated schools on college attendance, occupational choice and achievement, and voluntary interracial contact.

Although the studies are not entirely in agreement, in general it has been found that desegregation increased African-Americans' educational achievement and their willingness to interact with Whites in educational settings. African-Americans who attended desegregated high schools were more likely to finish high school, attend college, and earn higher GPAs while in college, and less likely to drop out of college, than African-Americans who attended segregated high schools (Braddock, Crain, & McPartland, 1984; Crain, Hawes, Miller, & Peichert, 1985; Crain & Mahard, 1978; Green, 1981; Wilson, 1979). The increase in college attendance rates appears to have occurred primarily in the North. In the South, African-Americans who attended desegregated high schools were more likely to attend traditionally all-White universities than were African-Americans who attended segregated high schools (Braddock, 1987; Braddock & McPartland, 1982).

Studies on occupational achievement have obtained mixed results, but on balance they suggest that school desegregation led to some improvements in the earnings of African-Americans (Braddock & McPartland, 1983; Crain, 1970; Crain & Straus, 1986; Crain & Weisman, 1972; U.S. Commission on Civil Rights, 1967). The results relating to attending desegregated colleges present a similar picture. The better-designed studies indicate that attendance at desegregated colleges enabled African-Americans to get better jobs compared with students attending segregated colleges (Braddock & McPartland, 1988). African-Americans are now represented in a greater variety of occupations than they were in the past (Farley, 1985; Pettigrew, 1979b), and it appears that desegregation played a role in this process (Crain, 1970; Crain et al., 1985).

The most consistent finding in the realm of intergroup relations is that African-Americans who attended desegregated schools are more likely to work in integrated environments as adults than are African-Americans who attended segregated schools (Astin, 1982; Braddock & McPartland, 1983). African-Americans from desegregated backgrounds also have more favorable evaluations of their White co-workers and bosses than do African-Americans from segregated backgrounds (Braddock & McPartland, 1983). In addition, African-Americans from desegregated backgrounds form more cross-racial friendships (Crain & Weisman, 1972; Ellison & Powers, 1994; Green, 1981). One study found that Whites who attended desegregated schools are also more likely to work in integrated settings (Braddock, McPartland, & Trent, 1984).

Both African-Americans and Whites who attended desegregated schools are more likely to live in integrated neighborhoods as adults and to send their children to desegregated schools than are African-Americans and Whites who attended segregated schools (Astin, 1982; Crain, 1970; U.S. Commission on Civil Rights, 1967). Desegregation also led to greater integration in housing when community-wide desegregation plans were adopted, because Whites could not easily avoid desegregation by moving to the suburbs (Braddock, Crain, & McPartland, 1984; Orfield, 1980; Pearce, 1980; Rossell, 1978).

The introduction of desegregation sometimes caused Whites to flee from newly desegregated school districts. White flight occurred primarily when desegregation plans required the reassignment of substantial numbers of White students in large, majority African-American, urban school districts surrounded by suburbs (Armor, 1980, 1988; U.S. Commission on Civil Rights, 1987). However, one long-term study of nine school districts that were desegregating in response to court orders concluded that desegregation had little effect on White flight (Smock & Wilson, 1991). When it did occur, White flight typically tapered off after the first year or so of desegregation (Rossell, 1978, cited in Armor, 1980;

U.S. Commission on Civil Rights, 1987; Wilson, 1985). Studies of parents suggest that desegregation did not lead to increases in opposition to desegregation among White parents (Rossell, 1978), and in a number of communities attitudes toward desegregation among parents became more positive as a result of desegregation (McConahay & Hawley, 1976; Parsons, 1986). A 1989 poll found that the majority of both White and African-American parents thought the desegregation experiences of their children were more than satisfactory (Harris & Associates, 1989). A 1994 Gallup poll indicated that 87% of Americans believed the Supreme Court's decision in *Brown* was right (*USA Today,* May 12, 1994). It appears that over time desegregation has become increasingly accepted in the United States (Orfield & Eaton, 1996).

In evaluating these results it should be kept in mind that the size of the effects in these studies was often relatively small, the number of studies is still not large, and the findings, while generally consistent across studies, do show some variability. Although the sample sizes in some studies were small, a number of these studies employed national samples and were considerably more comprehensive than the studies of the short-term effects of desegregation. Thus, while the results concerning the long-term effects of desegregation also should be regarded as tentative, they do appear to be generally stronger and more positive than those for the short-term effects.

In summary, the studies of the long-term effects of desegregation suggest that it led to some increases in educational and occupational attainment among African-Americans, and greater integration in colleges and universities, in the workplace, and in housing. It also contributed to changes in broader indices of race relations in the United States. On the negative side, desegregation led to some short-term increases in White flight.

Why were the long-term effects of desegregation generally more positive than the short-term effects? Although a complete answer to this question is not possible at this time, the following processes probably played a role. First, desegregation may provide African-Americans with knowledge of the norms, behaviors, and values of Whites that enables them to interact with Whites more effectively. Second, attending desegregated schools may foster interpersonal networks between African-Americans and Whites that help create access to higher-paying jobs in integrated settings (Braddock & McPartland, 1987; Crain & Weisman, 1972). Third, attending desegregated schools may lead African-Americans to believe that greater educational and occupational opportunities are available to them, which may cause them to apply for schools and jobs that students from segregated schools do not even attempt to apply for.

INSIGHTS FROM THE CONTACT MODEL

The contact model proposed earlier in this chapter is useful in appraising the effects of desegregation. This model would suggest that the societal context in which school desegregation took place, the characteristics of the participants, the situational factors, the mediators of change, and the long-term societal effects of contact should be considered if we wish to have a more complete understanding of the effects of desegregation (Rosenfield & Stephan, 1981).

School desegregation was designed as a legal remedy to the dual school systems of the American South in which African-Americans were provided with grossly inferior schools. These dual school systems were a historical legacy of slavery. Although the remedy was designed for the de jure segregated school systems of the South, it also was applied to the large urban de facto segregated schools of the North. It was enforced over the considerable opposition of (White) local school boards, administrators, teachers, and parents. It typically occurred amid a climate of controversy. Clearly, many of its architects hoped that it would change relations between the races, although it was not created specifically to do so (Stephan, 1978). It is against this backdrop that the effects of desegregation must be assessed.

The historical relations between African-Americans and Whites obviously affected the short-term lack of success of school desegregation in the United States, as did the fact that the two groups were unequal in socioeconomic and political status outside of the contact situation. Also, the two groups were, and are, dissimilar in a number of ways due to their different experiences in America. African-Americans were brought to this country as slaves, and had a different culture and religion from immigrant groups and the majority group (Pettigrew, 1986). They faced systematic, often legalized, discrimination and were not allowed to become assimilated into the mainstream culture as immigrant groups were. This history of interracial conflict meant that many White and African-American students entered the school situation with negative racial attitudes and stereotypes that were unlikely to lead to favorable outcomes.

There were also many situational factors that worked against improved intergroup relations in the schools, such as the fact that the

outcomes of intergroup contact in the schools frequently were not positive, the contact was nonvoluntary, and resegregation within schools
was common. A consideration of some of the mediators of the effects
of contact indicates further problems. The conditions of contact may
have led to categorical, rather than individual, processing of information and other information processing biases that worked against
changes in racial attitudes. Role models of positive intergroup contact
were often absent, as were rewards for positive contacts. And, outside
of the athletic field, Whites and African-Americans rarely cooperated
together in situations where they were interdependent.

The lack of short-term success of desegregation, along with the continuation of controversy over its implementation, contributed to the
gradual abandonment of school desegregation as a social policy. The
loss of public support and a succession of federal administrations that
lacked the political will to continue implementing it also contributed to
its demise (Orfield & Eaton, 1996). Nonetheless, school desegregation
has had a number of long-term effects on race relations in America. It
was one of the sparks that ignited the Civil Rights Movement. It also
brought into the public consciousness the issue of how society can
change race relations. In addition, desegregation played a role in changing Whites' attitudes toward African-Americans (Pettigrew, 1979a; Rossell, 1978). It affected the lives of hundreds of thousands of schoolchildren and provided them with exposure to members of other groups
that they would not have had otherwise. The effects of this exposure
will be felt, for good or ill, for years to come as these people move into
positions of leadership in this country. And, desegregation has affected
the mission of education in America. All schools, even those that were
never affected by desegregation, now acknowledge the importance of
addressing the issue of intergroup relations in some way in the curriculum, which was not true before desegregation and might not be true
now if it had not been for desegregation. This book might not exist if it
had not been for the movement to desegregate America's schools.

ADDITIONAL READINGS

Ben-Ari, R., & Rich, Y. (1997). *Enhancing education in heterogeneous schools.* Ra-
    mat-Gan, Israel: Bar-Ilan University Press.
Hewstone, M., & Brown, R. (Eds.). (1986). *Contact and conflict in intergroup en-
    counters.* Oxford: Basil Blackwell.
Miller, N., & Brewer, M. B. (Eds.). (1984). *Groups in contact: The psychology of
    desegregation.* Orlando, FL: Academic Press.

Orfield, G., & Eaton, S. F. (1996). *Dismantling desegregation*. New York: New Press.

Schofield, J. W. (1995). Review of research on school desegregation's impact on elementary and secondary students. In J. A. Banks & C. A. McGee Banks (Eds.), *Handbook of research on multicultural education* (pp. 257–314). New York: Macmillan.

Chapter 4

IMPROVING INTERGROUP RELATIONS

Few problems pose a greater threat to the future of our society than a continuation of our long history of racial and ethnic divisiveness. Currently, countervailing forces that promote improved intergroup relations (e.g., a concern with racial issues at the highest levels of the federal government) coexist alongside forces that foster their deterioration (e.g., resegregation in American cities, controversy over public policies that benefit minority groups), complicating the jobs of teachers who must function in schools buffeted by these forces. What can be done to improve intergroup relations in the schools?

In the past critics have argued, with considerable justification, that the social sciences understood more about the causes of stereotyping and prejudice than they did about improving intergroup relations. However, over the course of the past 2 decades much has been learned about techniques of reducing stereotyping and prejudice. In the discussion of this literature that follows, research on techniques of improving intergroup relations conducted in educational settings will be considered first. Next, two techniques developed in noneducational settings will be examined: cross-cultural training programs and conflict resolution techniques. Finally, several general issues relevant to the success of intergroup relations programs will be discussed. These issues include the manner in which the development of ethnic identity may affect programs designed to improve intergroup relations and the role of administrators in improving intergroup relations.

TECHNIQUES DEVELOPED FOR EDUCATIONAL SETTINGS

In the first two chapters I discussed the nature of the problems facing teachers who wish to reduce stereotyping and prejudice in their classrooms. In Chapter 3 I presented research on optimal intergroup contact situations and I examined the research on desegregation. Now, given this background information, what kind of program would you design to improve intergroup relations? Would you present students with information about other groups? How would you present this information and what information would you present? Would you integrate this material into your regular classes or would you suggest separate classes to cover this material? But just presenting information may not create the kinds of contact situations that research indicates are most helpful in improving relations between groups. What could you do to promote optimal intergroup contact in your classroom? And even if you could provide the best information and you could bring students from different groups into productive contact with one another, there will still be problems and conflicts between groups. What could you do to resolve these conflicts in ways that would promote better relations between groups? These are the issues that have faced the teachers and researchers who have designed programs to improve intergroup relations. In the next section of this chapter I will review four of the techniques they have developed: narrowly focused educational techniques, multicultural education, the use of cooperative learning groups, and moral development training programs.

Didactic Programs

Didactic programs focus on presenting information about intergroup relations in impactful and involving ways. Some of these techniques are designed to be used in programs of short duration and I will discuss these first. The goal of these programs is to provide students with brief experiences that will give them insights into stereotyping and prejudice, often by using role playing, group discussions, or simulation games. Other didactic programs are designed to be integrated into the entire school curriculum. They are intended to make intergroup relations a central focus of the students' educational experiences. I will discuss the more narrowly focused programs first and then turn to the more comprehensive programs.

Narrowly Focused Educational Programs. One of the root causes of prejudice is ignorance. Most educational programs that are designed to reduce prejudice are based on this premise. There is considerable justification in the research literature for the belief that reducing ignorance about other groups does reduce prejudice (McGregor, 1993; Stephan & Stephan, 1984). One review of education-oriented studies done prior to

1985 found that the majority (62%) of the studies reviewed (39) were successful in reducing prejudice (Stephan & Stephan, 1984). Similarly, McGregor's (1993) meta-analysis of 26 studies examining programs designed to reduce prejudice found that the majority were successful. McGregor (1993) also reported that a small number of studies suggested that prejudice reduction programs can boomerang and actually increase prejudice. Both reviews of the literature indicate that many well-meaning programs had no effects on intergroup relations. Stephan and Stephan (1984) concluded that programs including role playing were more effective than studies that focused primarily on teaching antiracist attitudes (e.g., Gray & Ashmore, 1975), but McGregor (1993) concluded that these two types of programs were equally effective. As this difference of opinion makes clear, we still do not know which kinds of programs are most successful and why.

Most of these didactic programs present students with readings, lectures, videos, movies, and demonstrations of music, dance, and other arts from different ethnic and cultural groups. Many of these programs also have employed more specific techniques designed to help students overcome prejudice and stereotyping. Specific techniques shown to be effective in these studies include stressing the positive similarities between groups (Kehoe & Rogers, 1978); learning about the norms, roles, and values of the other group (Triandis, 1975); dividing students into arbitrary groups and having them experience discrimination on the basis of this arbitrary distinction (Byrnes & Kiger, 1990; Weiner & Wright, 1973); writing essays supporting increased opportunities for minority groups (Gray & Ashmore, 1975); acting out cases of discrimination that can occur in school settings, such as making racially insensitive remarks or "jokes" or the use of racial epithets (Breckheimer & Nelson, 1976); role playing being a member of another group (Hohn, 1973; Kehoe & Rogers, 1978; Smith, 1990); negotiating agreements with a member of an outgroup (Thompson, 1993); having low-prejudiced children discuss their racial attitudes with high-prejudiced children (Aboud & Doyle, 1996); and keeping journals related to intergroup relations (Katz & Ivey, 1977). Unfortunately, little information is available concerning the relative efficacy of different techniques because so few studies have systematically compared their effectiveness. McGregor (1993) found that programs involving younger students (elementary and secondary school students) were generally more successful than those with older students, and that studies with lower teacher/student ratios showed the largest positive effects.

The primary problem with these programs is that they are narrowly focused, rather than comprehensive. They teach children about a particular ethnic group or impart a particular skill, but they fail to take into consideration the full complexity of intergroup relations in our society. The next program I will review, multicultural education, was specifically designed to be comprehensive.

Multicultural Education. One of the most widely used didactic programs is multicultural education (Banks, 1987, 1988, 1995b). Multicultural education is designed to teach students about the characteristics of the various ethnic groups that exist in our society—their similarities and differences, their histories and current experiences (Banks, 1987; Grant & Sleeter, 1989; NCSS Task Force, 1992). As Banks (1997) put it:

> An important goal of multicultural education is to improve race relations and to help all students acquire the knowledge, attitudes, and skills needed to participate in cross-cultural interactions in personal, social, and civic action that will help make our nation more democratic and just. (p. vii)

Instead of emphasizing the mainstream society, a multicultural curriculum reflects the views of different racial and ethnic minority groups. Students are presented with views and interpretations of their society from the perspectives of minority group members. Multicultural education is intended to be a comprehensive program that influences teaching and curricula across a broad range of content areas, including not only social studies, history, and language, but math, science, and the arts. Ideally multicultural education would involve sensitizing educators at all grade levels and in all areas to issues of cultural diversity in the classroom and in the curriculum. However, in practice, most of the multicultural curricula that have been developed are for social science, language, or history courses that last a semester or less. Curricula do exist, however, for students at many different age levels. The goal is to prepare students to "participate in public discourse and civic action with people who are different from them in significant ways" (NCSS Task Force, 1992, p. 274). The National Council for the Social Studies Task Force (1992) goes on to specify four goals with respect to ethnic and cultural diversity.

1. Ethnic and cultural diversity should be recognized and respected at the individual, group, and societal levels.
2. Ethnic and cultural diversity provides a basis for societal enrichment, cohesiveness, and survival.
3. Equality of opportunity should be afforded to members of all ethnic and cultural groups.

   4. Ethnic and cultural identification should be optional for individu-
      als. (p. 276)

   Another one of the explicit goals of multicultural education is prejudice reduction. The inclusion of multicultural materials in the curriculum is conceptually similar to many of the briefer intergroup relations
training programs, but multicultural education is potentially much
more powerful in its impact. The emphasis of multicultural education
programs on the history and culture of various ethnic groups, their
focus on the social construction of knowledge, and their attempts to
empower minority students and increase their achievement should all
improve intergroup relations (Banks, 1995b). Multicultural education's
orientation toward legitimizing all ethnic groups should facilitate the
formation of positive ethnic identities, as well as creating respect for
and acceptance of group differences. Unlike some of the other techniques of improving intergroup relations discussed in this chapter, extensive materials have been developed and now exist for classroom use
by teachers wishing to implement multicultural education (Banks, 1987,
1991, 1994; Dinnerstein, Nichols, & Reimers, 1996; Kendall, 1983; Ramsey, 1987; Sarocho & Spodek, 1983). These materials are full of detailed
instructions on how to teach students about intergroup relations. For
instance, Banks (1988), in discussing a curriculum that addresses con-
troversial issues in intergroup relations, suggests that teachers have
students research the views of civil rights activists of the 1960s (e.g.,
Martin Luther King, Jr., Stokely Carmichael, Julian Bond, Eldridge
Cleaver) and then hold a "convention" in which they discuss the attitudes of these figures toward racial integration versus segregation. Another exercise has students finish a set of unfinished sentences (e.g.,
"A racist is a person who . . .") and then discuss their answers in small
groups. A third exercise in this curriculum asks students to conduct
surveys in their schools or communities that would provide them with
information on various aspects of intergroup relations. Unfortunately,
there appear to be no systematic longitudinal studies of the impact of
multicultural education curricula on intergroup relations in the schools
(Sleeter & Grant, 1987).
   However, there have been a number of studies of the effects of training teachers in multicultural education. These studies suggest that exposure to short periods of multicultural instruction do not have much
of a long-term impact on preservice teachers. In contrast, longer and
more comprehensive programs do improve preservice and inservice
teachers' understanding of multicultural issues (Grant & Grant, 1985;
Grant & Tate, 1995; Noordhoff & Kleinfield, 1993). In particular, it has

been found that field experiences enhance preservice teachers' ability to work with ethnically diverse populations (Mahan, 1982, 1984). Unfortunately, there are also a number of reports of unsuccessful programs designed to help teachers learn multicultural concepts and integrate them into the curriculum (Grant & Tate, 1995; Sleeter, 1992). At this time, it is not clear why some teacher training programs are successful, whereas others are not.

Cooperative Learning Groups

Based on the principles developed in early studies of cooperation (Deutsch; 1949; Sherif et al., 1961), and the principles contained in the contact literature (Allport, 1954; Williams, 1947), several teams of researchers in different parts of the country have developed cooperative learning techniques designed to improve intergroup relations in school classrooms (Aronson, Blaney, Stephan, Sikes, & Snapp, 1978; Hertz-Lazarowitz & Miller, 1992; Johnson & Johnson, 1992a; Slavin, 1978; Weigel et al., 1975). These techniques use small cooperative learning groups composed of children from different racial and ethnic backgrounds. For example, in the peer-taught *jigsaw classroom* (Aronson et al., 1978; Aronson & Patnoe, 1997; Aronson & Thibodeau, 1992), the assigned material is divided into as many parts as there are students in the group. Each student then learns his or her own part of the material and presents this piece of the puzzle to the other members of the group. The students in each group are dependent on one another to learn all of the material. The groups do not compete with one another, and each student is graded individually on his or her performance. The groups usually meet for one class period a day for 4 to 6 weeks and then new groups are formed. There are a wide variety of related techniques currently in use in schools around the country (Bruffee, 1993; Cohen, 1992; Johnson, Johnson, & Holubec, 1994; Slavin, 1991). Here is a quote from one student on his experiences in a cooperative group.

> When we started to work in jigsaw groups, I began to realize that I wasn't really that stupid. And the kids I thought were cruel and hostile became my friends and the teacher acted so friendly and nice to me and I actually began to love school. (Aronson & Patnoe, 1997, p. 126)

The results of a number of studies using variations of cooperative learning teams indicate that the teams do improve intergroup relations. These studies have found that cross-ethnic helping and friendships increase (DeVries & Edwards, 1974; Johnson & Johnson, 1992b; Slavin,

1977, 1992; Weigel et al., 1975, Ziegler, 1981) and empathy and liking for other students increase (Blaney, Stephan, Rosenfield, Aronson, & Sikes, 1977; Bridgeman, 1977; for a review of the effects of cooperative learning techniques, see Johnson & Johnson, 1992a, 1992b). In addition, both the self-esteem and the achievement of minority students can be increased in cooperative groups (Blaney et al., 1977; DeVries, Edwards, & Slavin, 1978; Johnson & Johnson, 1992a, 1992b; Lucker, Rosenfield, Aronson, & Sikes, 1977; Sharan & Shachar, 1988), although achievement gains are not always found (Slavin, 1990). Nearly all of the studies cited above were conducted in the United States, but cooperative techniques have been used with similar positive effects in Israel (Hertz-Lazarowitz, Sapir, & Sharan, 1982; Shachar & Amir, 1996; Sharan & Shachar, 1988).

A variety of factors appear to be operating together to produce these favorable results. Working in cooperative groups tends to undercut ingroup/outgroup bias. Ingroup/outgroup bias is based on identification with the ethnic ingroup and rejection of outgroups. When students work together in mixed teams, they come to identify with and favorably evaluate their own team, which contains members of both the ethnic ingroup and outgroups. The teams thus become superordinate groups in which initial distinctions between ethnic groups are submerged (cf. Gaertner et al., 1990; Gaertner et al., 1989).

Interaction with outgroup members in cooperative groups also provides students with an opportunity to acquire information that is inconsistent with their stereotypes. This disconfirming information can change stereotypes because it occurs frequently, for a variety of outgroup members, and across many different situations (cf. Rothbart & John, 1985). The students also learn that outgroup members vary considerably, which can lead to differentiated perceptions of the outgroup. In addition, in this context the students are dependent on one another, and dependence leads to an increased focus on individuating information (Erber & Fiske, 1984).

Being interdependent has other benefits as well. After reviewing over 600 studies on cooperative learning groups, one set of researchers argue that mutual interdependence leads people in cooperative groups to put aside their own immediate interests in favor of striving to help all members of the group achieve their joint goals (Johnson & Johnson, 1992a). The students take pride in the accomplishments of others and become bound to them by ties of mutual obligation and responsibility, leading to feelings of cohesion and attraction to other group members.

One potential problem for cooperative learning groups is that the majority group students are often higher in social class and achievement level than the minority students. Cohen (1980) and her co-workers have found, however, that even these status inequalities can be overcome if the minority students are highly competent on at least some of the assigned tasks. In her earlier studies she trained minority group members to explicitly disconfirm negative stereotypes concerning minority competence (they were provided with technical skills so that they could quickly assemble a radio). She found that this training subsequently led to more equal-status relationships between Whites and African-Americans. In her more recent work, Cohen has developed a technique she calls the Program for Complex Instruction (Cohen, 1990; Cohen et al., 1994). In this program, students work in small mixed groups on tasks that require a variety of skills (intellectual, spatial, artistic, dramatic, etc.). In order to take advantage of the fact that different students excel at different skills, the students are rotated through roles requiring a variety of skills so that they all have opportunities to display their particular talents. Her studies indicate that these classrooms lead to increased acceptance of lower-status (usually minority) students and increased achievement (Cohen, 1986, 1990).

In another solution to the status inequality problem, each student's performance contributes to the team's overall standing (DeVries & Edwards, 1974). To ensure that low-achieving students do not hinder the team, the students in each team receive points on the basis of comparisons with other students at their own achievement level. In this way, low-achieving students help or hinder their team no more than high-achieving students do (Slavin, 1992). This solution to the status inequality problem makes it unlikely that low-ability students will be blamed if the team performs poorly (cf. Rosenfield et al., 1981).

Given the beneficial effects of cooperative groups on intergroup relations, it is puzzling that they have not been more widely adopted in public schools in the United States. Various answers to this puzzle have been advanced by researchers in this area (Cohen, 1990; Deutsch, 1993; Johnson & Johnson, 1995b). One answer is that these techniques require extensive teacher training and organizational support. Unfortunately, most teachers are not trained to use these techniques as a part of their college education. Also, many teachers believe in myths about cooperative learning that undercut their willingness to employ these techniques (Johnson & Johnson, 1995b). Teachers frequently believe that cooperative groups do not adequately prepare students for the competitive nature of the adult world of business. In addition, some teachers believe that high-achieving students are penalized in cooperative learning programs, that the grading is unfair, and that some students do all the work while others do little or none. These myths have been refuted by Deutsch (1993) and Johnson and Johnson (1995b).

They argue that cooperation is an essential skill, even in the highly competitive field of business, and it is especially important for building and maintaining strong families, friendships, and communities. High-achieving students frequently learn more in cooperative than in competitive classrooms because teaching less able students solidifies their knowledge. The grading need not be unfair, since students can be graded individually or against peers at their own ability level. Finally, cooperative groups make it difficult for less motivated students to get a free ride because there is considerable social pressure for all students to contribute. Less motivated students frequently are drawn into contributing more than they ordinarily would.

Moral Development Training Programs

Davidson and Davidson (1994) argue that moral development programs that are based on Kohlberg's (1969, 1981) theory of moral development, and that include discussions of group differences in perceptions, backgrounds, and cultures, raise the level of children's moral reasoning and improve intergroup relations. Empirical studies have shown that dramatizing moral dilemmas and role-playing exercises increase children's levels of moral reasoning (Blatt & Kohlberg, 1975). Among the specific techniques that Davidson and Davidson (1994) recommend to improve intergroup relations in elementary schools are describing social practices in different groups and noting the similar values underlying them, creating booklets of family history or maps of family origins, arranging visits to the class by representatives of various groups, playing tape recordings of older relatives, and role playing or brief dramas using racial or ethnic themes.

At the high school level, the "Facing History and Ourselves" program uses an examination of the Holocaust to sensitize students to anti-Semitism and a host of related issues (Stoskopf & Strom, 1990). The "Facing History" curriculum is designed to be a one-semester, history-related course (Fine, 1993, 1995). It focuses on a particular historical period, Nazi Germany before and during World War II, but guides the students to use these historical incidents to reflect on the present-day problems of prejudice and racism. The curriculum materials also encourage students to analyze their own values and identities as they analyze the Holocaust. The concluding segments of the curriculum address students' responsibility for protecting civil liberties. The goals of this program are to foster perspective taking, critical thinking, and moral decision making. The materials are presented in a way that is relevant to the students' own experiences of prejudice and stereotyping. For instance, after reading an assigned novel about discrimination against Jews in Nazi Germany, students in one class were given an assignment to write about situations where they had witnessed similar acts of discrimination (Fine, 1993). One student wrote:

> I was with a friend once and someone else who thought I was a friend called that person a "greasy spic." I felt sorry for the person who said it because anyone who is that proud of their ignorance deserves some amount of sympathy. The power of words simply means that spoken words can hurt or heal depending on how you use them. (Fine, 1993, p. 780)

Unfortunately, few of these moral education programs have been systematically evaluated, and their effects on intergroup relations, although they seem obvious, appear never to have been tested. If these techniques are successful, it is most likely because they succeed in inculcating universal moral values such as a concern for the welfare for all people, and concerns for social justice, equality, and peace. One recent study of Israeli teachers indicates that subscribing to these universal values was associated with low levels of prejudice toward Arabs (Sagiv & Schwartz, 1995), which lends credence to the idea that promoting these values would reduce prejudice.

TECHNIQUES DEVELOPED IN NONEDUCATIONAL SETTINGS

A great deal of the research on techniques of improving intergroup relations has focused on settings other than the schools. Some of most interesting techniques were designed to train people in intercultural relations, that is, to train people who are going abroad to work or study. Another intriguing set of techniques consist of procedures to resolve intergroup conflicts. These techniques, too, initially were designed for use in international settings, but more recently they also have been applied to both work and school settings.

Cross-Cultural Training Programs

Although it might seem that programs designed to prepare people to adjust to foreign cultures are not relevant to efforts to improve intergroup relations domestically, they are worth reviewing because they do improve relations between groups. These programs are designed to: (1) improve the social skills involved in interacting with people who are different from one's own group, (2) increase feelings of comfort in such interactions, (3) improve relationships with people from the other group, (4) increase the accuracy of intergroup perceptions, and (5) reduce intergroup misunderstandings (Brislin & Yoshida, 1994). All of these goals are relevant to improving domestic intergroup relations in the schools.

A review of 29 evaluation studies done prior to 1990 shows that these programs were almost always successful (Black & Mendenhall, 1990). For instance, 10 studies employing appropriate control groups found that intercultural training improved relationship skills relevant to intercultural relations; 14 studies using control groups found that the training led to more accurate perceptions of the other culture; and seven of the studies employing control groups found that the training improved adjustment to the new culture.

The most effective programs are those that emphasize laboratory and field simulations, role playing (including critiques of performance), exercises to increase general or country-specific cultural sensitivity, case studies, sensitivity training, interactions with "old hands" from the trainee's own culture who have had extensive experience in the culture in question, field trips, cultural immersion, and interactions with individuals from the other culture (Bhawuk, 1990; Brislin, Landis, & Brandt, 1983; Gudykunst & Hammer, 1983). Role playing simulations such as the Contrast American and BAFA–BAFA provide examples of the type of experiential training exercises commonly used in these programs. The Contrast American exercise was developed by the military to train people for foreign service. In this exercise, an American trainee interacts with a contrast-American trainer, who portrays an individual whose values and assumptions contrast with those of the typical American (Stewart, 1966; Stewart, Danielian, & Foster, 1969). BAFA–BAFA has long been used to train Peace Corps volunteers. In this simulation, American trainees interact with each other in a structured situation as if they were from cultures with values and assumptions different from those of Americans (Shirts, 1973). One "culture" is a patriarchal culture that values developing friendships through established ritual, while the other is an egalitarian culture that values accumulating points through bargaining. These experiential techniques have been recommended as additions to information-based programs (Bhawuk, 1990; Brislin et al., 1983; Gudykunst & Hammer, 1983). The primary advantage of experiential techniques is that active training is more involving and realistic than more passive didactic programs. In addition, trainees receive experience in problem solving, and they have the opportunity to test their capabilities.

One of the best known cross-cultural training techniques is the cultural sensitizer (Cushner & Landis, 1996; Triandis, 1972). When using this technique, participants read 75–100 incidents concerning cultural differences between their culture and the other culture. Each incident employs a multiple choice response format in which the participants select the solution to the problem that reflects their understanding of the issues involved. When they select wrong answers, the reasons why the answers are wrong are explained to them, and when they select the correct answer, the cultural difference that makes this answer correct is explained to them. A variety of studies indicate that this technique is successful in teaching members of one group to better understand the culture of other groups (e.g., Cushner, 1989; Landis, Brislin, & Hulgus, 1985; Landis, Day, McGrew, Thomas, & Miller, 1976; Weldon et al., 1975). This technique has now been used to train a wide variety of groups and with subjects of various ages (Cushner & Landis, 1996).

From the perspective of domestic intergroup relations, the most fascinating aspect of intercultural relations programs is the underlying assumption that the focus of training should be on differences between groups, not their similarities. The premise is obvious from the intercultural perspective—it is the differences between groups that create misunderstandings and conflicts—but it contrasts with many domestic intergroup relations training programs that focus on the similarities between groups. When translated into the domestic context, the intercultural relations approach suggests that students should be taught the differences among groups in way that creates respect and tolerance for group differences in customs, traditions, and norms. Any real similarities between the groups also should be pointed out, and attempts should be made to dispel myths about differences that do not exist. One major value of this approach is that the goal is not to produce assimilation, but to further pluralism by honoring group differences. The risk of any approach that emphasizes differences, of course, is that these differences will be evaluated negatively and used to reinforce stereotyping and justify prejudice.

Conflict Resolution Techniques

Small conflict resolution workshops consisting of members of opposing groups can be used to foster mutual understanding. Researchers from Harvard, Yale, and the University of London pioneered this approach (Burton, 1974, 1987; Doob, 1974; Kelman, 1990; Kelman & Cohen, 1986; Rouhana & Kelman, 1994), which brings together members of conflicting groups with a group facilitator. The group facilitator presents the conflict as a problem to be solved, not a contest to be won, and fosters a norm of analytical processing concerning the various aspects of the conflict. The participants are encouraged to express their feelings, hopes, and fears. They also engage in role taking so they can learn to take the views of both sides into consideration when discussing solutions. The ultimate goal is to feed new ideas and changed perceptions into relations between the groups.

Conflict resolution workshops have been used to facilitate the resolution of a wide variety of conflicts. A particularly interesting workshop was conducted with Blacks, Coloreds, and Whites in South Africa using individuals who worked for the same large corporation (Kamfer & Venter, 1994). The goal of this workshop was to enable these groups to work together effectively, despite the ethnic diversity that existed in the workplace. Mixed groups of about 25 people met for 2 days to discuss intergroup relations. The groups spent much of their time together exploring issues of racial identity, stereotyping, and discrimination. Toward the end of the workshop the participants discussed techniques of dealing with everyday racial conflict situations and how to apply these techniques in their jobs and lives. Research indicates that these workshops reduced stereotyping (Kamfer & Venter, 1994). Another example is provided by a workshop conducted to facilitate resolution of a conflict between Turkish and Greek Cypriots (Fisher, 1994). The workshop dealt with the needs and fears of each side and assisted them in providing assurances to each other to assuage those fears. The parties reached a consensus on the desired qualities of a renewed relationship. The participants also reported that the workshops increased understanding and mutual empathy. Although there is relatively little empirical evidence on the effectiveness of these techniques, it has been suggested that they produce a more complex and subtle view of the other side, aid in identifying destructive interpretations of the actions of the other side, and facilitate the design of effective solutions (Ross, 1993).

The use of mediation to resolve conflicts in school settings has received increasing attention from theorists and practitioners in the past decade (Johnson & Johnson, 1995a, 1995b; Johnson, Johnson, Dudley, & Magnusson, 1995). Programs designed to improve the conflict resolution skills of students have been conducted in a number of school systems around the country (Araki, 1990; Johnson, Johnson, Dudley, & Acikgoz, 1994; Tolson, McDonald, & Moriarity, 1992). For example, one program was created for inner-city high schools in New York City. It was found that the conflict resolution training improved students' abilities to manage conflict, increased their social support from other students, and decreased victimization by others (Deutsch, 1993). The students also experienced increases in self-esteem, decreases in anxiety, and greater feelings of self-control. Another study, this one using elementary students, found that 9 hours of mediation training led to the successful acquisition of mediation skills as measured in hypothetical conflict situations (Johnson et al., 1995). Although these programs were not designed specifically to improve intergroup relations, the skills that were acquired are clearly relevant to resolving intergroup conflicts.

After interviewing professional mediators of intergroup conflicts, Coleman and Deutsch (1995) offered a series of suggestions for dealing with such conflicts in school settings. They argue that introducing conflict mediation curricula in schools creates a climate in which students are more willing to voluntarily submit their conflicts to resolution. They believe that it is important to have mediators from all of the contending parties, but if this is not possible the mediators should be trusted by all parties. They assert that students trained in mediation can be effective mediators for peer conflicts. They stress that the focus of mediation should be on future solutions, rather than on past blame. They suggest that the disputants be allowed to vent their emotions, but advise that mediators should be aware of cultural differences in the manner in which emotions are expressed. Mediators also should help all the parties to become aware of the ways in which their cultural backgrounds have shaped their views of the conflict and of the other parties.

ISSUES THAT HAVE AN IMPACT ON
INTERGROUP RELATIONS IN THE SCHOOLS

The success of all of these techniques depends on the situational context in which they are introduced. School policies and characteristics that have an impact on intergroup relations, including tracking, disciplinary policies, parental involvement, and the racial composition of the staff, can affect the success of intergroup relations programs. Likewise, the racial composition of the student body, and the degree to which the students identify with their racial or ethnic groups, can affect the outcomes of intergroup relations programs. These important issues are discussed in the following section.

School Policies Affecting Intergroup Relations

One aspect of the social culture that exists within schools that can have an impact on the outcomes of intergroup relations programs is segregation by group (Schofield, 1995). Students from different groups often segregate themselves in the lunchroom, in classrooms, and in their extracurricular activities (Braddock, Dawkins, & Wilson, 1995; Schofield, 1995). In addition, tracking students by academic ability often has the unintended effect of segregating students by ethnic group, as well as stigmatizing the students in the lower tracks (Braddock & Slavin, 1993; Epstein, 1985). Schools can take active measures to counter some aspects of within-school segregation, such as the elimination of tracking, and a number of studies suggest that doing so improves intergroup relations (Crain, Mahard, & Narot, 1982; Hallinan & Teixeira, 1987; Slavin & Madden, 1979).

Another area of school policy that is relevant to intergroup relations is disciplinary actions. If disciplinary actions fall disproportionately on minority group students and are perceived as unfair, intergroup relations are likely to suffer.

Teacher training may be one of the most important components of improving intergroup relations in the schools (Zeichner, 1995). Studies of preservice training of teachers in the techniques of multicultural education indicate that this training can have a positive impact on the teachers' "ability to work with ethnically diverse students" (Grant & Tate, 1995). Teachers need extensive training in understanding the backgrounds of the students they teach, as well as knowledge about how to present issues of racism, stereotyping, prejudice, and discrimination to their students. Banks (1995a) believes that the teachers who are most likely to be effective in improving intergroup relations possess democratic attitudes, a multiethnic philosophy, a capacity to take the role of members of other ethnic groups, an understanding of the multidimensional nature of ethnicity, and an awareness of their own ethnic attitudes, behaviors, and perceptions.

Parents, too, can have an impact on the outcomes of programs designed to improve intergroup relations, although their role may not always be a positive one. For instance, research indicates that children of parents who have negative intergroup attitudes tend to avoid intergroup contact (Patchen, 1982). Enlisting parental support for intergroup relations programs almost certainly would increase their effectiveness. McGee Banks (1993/1995) offers a number of suggestions for getting parents more involved in the education of their children, which would seem to apply to enlisting their support for intergroup relations programs. For instance, she suggests that teachers invite parents into their classrooms, write to parents or talk to them on the telephone, become involved in the community, and solicit the parents' views on educational goals for their children.

Although changing the curriculum is the major thrust of multicultural educational programs, Banks (1995a) also argues that all schools have implicit curricula that have an impact on race relations. The implicit curricula concern the lessons that no teacher explicitly teaches, but that all students learn. It is embedded in school policies and the communities in which schools function. The implicit curricula are communicated by such practices as the way teachers treat majority and minority group members, and boys and girls; how teachers respond to the languages and dialects that their students use; the racial effects of grouping practices within the schools; power relationships among administrators, teachers, and students; the attitudes toward ethnic diversity that exist in the schools; the texts chosen for use in the schools; and the types of learning styles the schools accommodate. The implicit curricula can encourage or discourage favorable intergroup relations. Many schools could improve their intergroup relations climate by examining and rectifying implicit curricular practices that communicate negative messages concerning relations between groups.

Identity Issues

One of the major dilemmas any attempt to improve intergroup relations must confront is whether to emphasize group differences in order to create positive ingroup identities or to de-emphasize group differences in the interests of being "color-blind." Social identity theorists have shown that strong identification with the ingroup may be accompanied by greater discrimination in favor of that group (Tajfel, 1978, 1981; Tajfel & Turner, 1979, 1986). However, several studies have found that individuals who have the greatest pride in their own groups are the least prejudiced toward outgroups (Aboud & Doyle, 1993; Gonzales & Cauce, 1995). The latter studies suggest that it is possible to have strong, positive identification with an ethnic ingroup without necessarily creating hostility toward outgroups. Clearly, creating such identities would be desirable, but it also may be difficult.

Cross (1995) has discussed aspects of this dilemma as they apply to African-Americans. He warns that many young people in the African-American underclass have adopted an "oppositional" identity (Fordham & Ogbu, 1986). The essence of this identity is that "if Whites are perceived to act one way, Black is its reverse" (Cross, 1995, p. 191). If Whites are thought to be polite, but evasive, then African-Americans will wish to be blunt and confrontational, according to this formulation. In the case of oppositional identities, positive identity clearly is purchased at the cost of outgroup rejection. Undercutting oppositional identities is a formidable task.

In creating positive identities, Cross (1995) emphasizes three aspects of African-American identity: defending against the stresses created by racism, creating a sense of purpose and a feeling of affiliation with African-Americans, and facilitating social relations with other groups. He suggests that because African-Americans live in a society with a long history of racism, they must acknowledge the existence of racism, be equipped with techniques of coping with racism that avoid self-blame, and learn to recognize the role of systemic or structural factors as causes of racism. The hazard in teaching these ideas is that it will create hostility toward the majority group and thus cause a deterioration, not an improvement, in intergroup relations.

More generally, Cross and other theorists have argued that minority and majority group members go through a series of stages in the development of their ethnic identities (Ponterotto & Pedersen, 1993; Smith, 1991). Ponterotto and Pedersen (1993) suggest that the development of ethnic identity may differ for students from majority and minority groups. For minority groups they suggest that there are four stages in the development of ethnic identities: (1) identification with the White majority; (2) awareness, encounter, and search; (3) identification and immersion; and (4) integration and internalization. Identification with the White majority can occur even in the absence of extensive contact with the majority group. During this stage individuals actually may hold less positive attitudes toward their own group than toward the White majority. The second stage involves a questioning of this identification with the White majority. Entry into this stage often occurs as a consequence of encountering discrimination at the hands of the majority group and may involve considerable confusion about ethnic identity. Prejudice toward the majority group may emerge during this stage, but it is unlikely to be accompanied by discrimination. In the third stage individuals become immersed in the customs of their own group, while rejecting those of Whites. Intense emotions and strong prejudices, as well as discrimination against Whites, may occur during this stage. In the fourth stage a re-assessment of identity takes place and a more balanced view emerges. Ethnic identity at this stage is secure and prejudice toward other groups is attenuated.

For the majority group Ponterotto and Pedersen (1993) argue that there are five stages of identity development: (1) pre-exposure; (2) conflict; (3) antiracism; (4) retreat into White culture; and (5) redefinition and integration. During stage 1 Whites have not begun to explore their ethnic identity, but there is an unconscious identification with being White. There is also an unquestioning acceptance of the stereotypes of minority groups. In stage 2 Whites begin to examine their own cultural values. They may experience some confusion and guilt over White racism and they typically wish to adhere to nonracist values. Many Whites respond to their growing understanding of racism by becoming actively antiracist in stage 3. However, attitudes toward minority groups may still be paternalistic at this stage. In stage 4 the Whites who did not respond to stage 3 by adopting antiracist attitudes typically retreat into White culture and may experience fear and anger with regard to minority group members. In stage 5 Whites make a transition to a more balanced ethnic identity. Whites in this stage are more flexible and open in their intergroup relations.

The ethnic identity development stage theories suffer from a variety of drawbacks that somewhat limit their utility. It is not clear in these theories that the stages are truly sequential or that all children go through them. These theories may be most useful as descriptions of some of the possible developmental phases that children may experience as they grow and learn about their own group and other groups. It is possible that some stages may not occur at all for many students, and it may be impossible to categorize some students using these stages.

The goal of most intergroup relations programs will be to facilitate movement toward the highest stage of ethnic identity proposed by these models. Clearly, teachers employing intergroup relations programs need to be aware of the nature of the ethnic identities that characterize the students in their classes. A knowledge of the identity stages of both minority and majority group members should be useful in determining what techniques to use, since some techniques are likely to be more effective with students at a given stage than at others. Students who have adopted oppositional identities pose particular problems that teachers will need to address before improvements in intergroup relations can occur. The fact that many student populations will have individuals at various stages of identity clearly complicates the teacher's task. It also may explain why some programs fail with some students, since the programs may not be suited to heterogeneous groups of students.

One additional point needs to be made here concerning racial and ethnic identity. Although it is commonly thought that children of mixed heritage have difficulty establishing positive racial or ethnic identities, this does not appear to be the case. Many students of mixed heritage have flexible ethnic identities, identifying with one aspect of their heritage in some situations and with other aspects in other situations (Root, 1992; Stephan & Stephan, 1989a). Others identify with both components of their heritage most of the time. Thus, their identities are often fluid, rather than firm, but that does not mean that their identities are not positive. Another misconception is that students of mixed heritage suffer from mental problems. Being raised in a multicultural home also does not appear to have any negative effects on mental health (Johnson & Nagoshi, 1986; Stephan & Stephan, 1991). Thus, there is little reason to think that mixed-heritage students cannot develop healthy, positive racial or ethnic identities. It is unlikely that the stage theories developed for minority and majority groups apply directly to students of mixed heritage.

CONCLUSION

One of the great shortcomings of the literature on programs designed to improve intergroup relations is that only a few of these programs have been tested rigorously (e.g., cooperative learning groups). An enormous number of such programs are in existence, but too little is known about the effects of some of them, including multicultural education, moral education programs, and conflict mediation training. Basically, our knowledge about what works, and why, is still limited. One of the most valuable investments that could be made in our understanding of techniques of improving intergroup relations would be to conduct systematic evaluations of these programs. Conducting evaluations is not easy, but in the absence of evaluation research, enormous amounts of money, time, and human effort will be wasted on programs that may be of little or no benefit.

Whatever programs are created to improve intergroup relations, it is important to have them systematically evaluated. Such an evaluation would require that students in these programs be pretested and posttested using the same set of instruments. The details of the techniques used in each program would have to be recorded carefully, along with the age of the participants, the ethnic composition of the students, the duration of the program, and so on. These types of evaluations would make it possible to determine what types of programs and techniques are most effective for which types of populations—information that is much needed, but currently unavailable. If you are not in a position to evaluate a change program that you wish to institute, you might consider contacting the closest university and seeing if you can interest professors or graduate students in education or psychology in evaluating the program.

For many years educators could claim that there were few techniques of improving intergroup relations available so there was not much they could do in this area. The research reviewed above suggests that this is no longer the case—social scientists have developed a number of promising programs to reduce prejudice and stereotyping. The task that remains for the future is to encourage teachers to adopt, amend, and assess these techniques.

ADDITIONAL READINGS

Akin, T. (1995). *Character education in America's schools.* Spring Valley, CA: Inner-choice Publishing (PO Box 2476, Spring Valley, CA 91979).

Aronson, E., & Patnoe, S. (1997). *The jigsaw classroom.* New York: Longman.

Banks, J. A. (1994). *An introduction to multicultural education* (3rd ed.). Boston: Allyn & Bacon.

Banks, J. A. (1997). *Educating citizens in a multicultural society.* New York: Teachers College Press.

Banks, J. A., & Clegg, A. A. (1990). *Teaching strategies for social studies: Theory and practice* (4th ed.). New York: Longman.

Bowers, V., & Swanson, D. (1988). *More than meets the eye.* Vancouver: Pacific Educational Press.

Bowser, B. P., Auletta, G. S., & Jones, T. (1993). *Confronting diversity issues on campus.* Newbury Park, CA: Sage.

Brislin, R. W., & Yoshida, T. (Eds.). (1994). *Improving intercultural interaction programs.* Thousand Oaks, CA: Sage.

Bruffee, K. A. (1993). *Collaborative learning.* Baltimore: Johns Hopkins University Press.

Burke, B. (1995). *Celebrate our similarities.* Huntington Beach, CA: Teacher Created Materials (PO Box 1040, 92647).

Cech, M. (1991). *Globalchild: Multicultural resources for young children.* Menlo Park, CA: Addison-Wesley.

Cohen, E. G. (1992). *Restructuring the classroom: Conditions for productive small groups.* Madison: Wisconsin Center for Education Research.

Cohen, J. J., & Fish, M. C. (1993). *Handbook of school based interventions.* San Francisco: Jossey-Bass.

Cushner, K., & Brislin, R. (1996). *Intercultural interaction: A practical guide* (2nd ed.). Thousand Oaks, CA: Sage.

Davidson, F. H., & Davidson, M. M. (1994). *Changing childhood prejudice: The caring work of the schools.* Westport, CT: Greenwood Press.

Derman-Sparks, L. (1995). *Anti-bias curriculum: Tools for empowering children.* Washington, DC: National Association for the Education of Young Children.

Diaz, C. E. (Ed.). (1992). *Multicultural education for the 21st century.* Washington, DC: National Education Association.

Fine, M. (1995). *Habits of mind: Struggling over values in America's classrooms.* San Francisco: Jossey-Bass.

Fowler, S. M., & Mumford, M. G. (1995). *Intercultural sourcebook: Cross-cultural training methods* (Vol. 1). Yarmouth, ME: Intercultural Press.

Halstead, J. M., & Taylor, M. J. (1996). *Values in education and education in values.* Bristol, PA: Falmer Press.

Hawley, W. D., & Jackson, A. W. (Eds.). (1995). *Toward a common destiny: Improving race and ethnic relations in America.* San Francisco: Jossey-Bass.

Johnson, D. W., & Johnson, R. T. (1995). *My mediation notebook* (3rd ed.). Edina, MN: Interaction Book Co.

Johnson, D. W., & Johnson, R. T. (1995). *Teaching students to be peacemakers* (3rd ed.). Edina, MN: Interaction Book Co.

Johnson, D. W., Johnson, R., & Holubec, E. J. (1994). *Circles of learning: Cooperation in the classroom* (4th ed.). Edina, MN: Interaction Book Co.

Jones, J. M. (1998). *The cultural psychology of African-Americans.* Boulder, CO: Westview.

Kohls, L. R., & Knight, J. M. (1994). *Developing intercultural awareness.* Yarmouth, ME: Intercultural Press.

Landis, D., & Bhagat, R. S. (1996). *Handbook of intercultural training.* Thousand Oaks, CA: Sage.

Looking for America: Vol. 1. Promising school based practices in intergroup relations. (1994). Boston: National Coalition of Advocates for Students (100 Boyston St. Suite 737, Boston, MA 02116).

Parker, W. M., Archer, J., & Scott, J. (1992). *Multicultural relations on campus.* Muncie, IN: Accelerated Development.

Power, F. C., Higgins, A., & Kohlberg, L. (Eds.). (1989). *Lawrence Kohlberg's approach to moral education.* New York: Columbia University Press.

Rothenberg, P. S. (Ed.). (1997). *Race, class, and gender* (4th ed.). New York: St. Martin's Press.

Seelye, H. N. (Ed.). (1996). *Experiential activities for intercultural learning.* Yarmouth, MA: Intercultural Press.

Seelye, H. N., & Wasilewski, H. (1996). *Between cultures: Developing self-identity in a world of diversity.* Yarmouth, ME: Intercultural Press.

Simon, K. T., et al. (1996). *Lessons on equal worth and dignity.* New York: United Nations Association of the United States of America (485 Fifth Ave. 10017-6104).

Slavin, R. E. (1991). *Student team learning: A practical guide to cooperative learning.* Washington, DC: National Education Association.

Stahl, R. J. (Ed.). (1994). *Cooperative learning in social studies: A handbook for teachers.* Menlo Park, CA: Addison-Wesley.

Thomson, B. J. (1992). *Words can hurt you: Beginning a program of anti-bias education.* Reading, MA: Addison-Wesley.

Also search ERIC and PSYCHLIT on cd-rom in the reference section of most university libraries for up-to-date materials on intergroup relations and related topics. Many of the materials on ERIC can be ordered from the ERIC Clearinghouse.

RESOURCES

Films for the Humanities and Sciences has a wide range of films and videos on
multicultural themes. PO Box 2053, Princeton, NJ 08543-2053 (800-257-
5126).

Blue-Eyed. A video of Jane Elliot's blue-eyed/brown-eyed diversity training technique. Resolution Inc., 149 Ninth St., San Francisco, CA 94103 (415-621-
6196). They also have other videos on diversity issues.

For other videos on multicultural education, contact Insight Videos, 2162
Broadway, New York, NY 10024-6620 (212-721-6316).

Center for Teaching Peace, 4501 Van Ness St. NW, Washington, DC 20016.

Educators for Social Responsibility, 23 Garden St., Cambridge, MA 02138.

Facing History and Ourselves, 25 Kennard Rd., Brookline, MA 02146.

The Grace Cotrino Abrams Peace Education Foundation, 3550 Biscayne Blvd.
Suite 400, Miami, FL 33137.

Human Rights Resource Center, 615 B St., San Rafael, CA 94901.

National Association for Mediation in Education, 425 Amity St., Amherst, MA
01002.

The Southern Poverty Law Center, 400 Washington Ave., Montgomery, AL 36104.

Chapter 5

RECOMMENDATIONS FOR INTERGROUP RELATIONS PROGRAMS

No one intergroup relations program can solve the problems of intergroup relations in American schools. The reason is that every school district is different, every school is unique, and every class is a world unto itself. The solutions have to be tailored to fit the problems that exist in that district, school, and classroom. It is easier to sketch out the goals of intergroup relations programs than it is to specify means of achieving these goals that would apply to all cases. The goals are to create students who understand and respect the differences between groups and are aware of the underlying similarities; recognize their own biases, as well as those of others; treat others as individuals, while recognizing the important role racial, ethnic, and other groups play in our lives; are firm in their own identities and are comfortable with other students who are firm in theirs; are able to interact effectively and productively with people who differ from them; value equality, justice, freedom, respect, dignity, and compassion; and understand the history of racial division in our society and are committed to overcoming it. It is up to teachers to design and implement specific programs and practices that will achieve these and related goals in their own particular contexts.

In this chapter I offer some recommendations for programs designed to improve intergroup relations in the schools. These recommendations are derived from the social science literature on intergroup relations, particularly research on the contact hypothesis and intergroup relations programs. Many of these recommendations have been subjected to systematic tests, but some are speculations based on theory or practical experience and have not yet been tested.

I will offer recommendations in four domains. The first domain is concerned with social information processing, specifically, categorization, stereotyping, and emotional responses to outgroup members. This domain of issues is primarily psychological and deals largely with cognitive processes at the individual level. The second domain concerns values and value-related issues such as the value placed on group identity. This domain concerns group issues and is directed toward creating beliefs that promote self-acceptance and the acceptance of others. The third domain concerns the development of intergroup relations skills. In this domain the emphasis is on the acquisition of behaviors that increase competence in intergroup interactions. The fourth domain deals with the social culture of the schools. The premise for this last domain of recommendations is the idea that it is easier to change the thoughts, values, and behavior of students when the social milieu of the school supports these changes. All of the recommendations focus primarily on stereotyping and prejudice.

First, a few caveats. Although some of these recommendations can be implemented only in situations where intergroup contact is possible, others can be implemented even in classes containing members of only one ethnic or racial group. Some of the recommendations are best implemented in programs designed specifically to improve intergroup relations, while others are more general recommendations regarding changes in the social culture of the schools themselves. Although it is possible to implement some of these recommendations in short-term programs, all of them are likely to be more effective if they are incorporated into long-term intergroup relations programs. Unfortunately, the majority of the studies on which these recommendations are based examined short-term programs lasting less than 6 weeks and sometimes less than a day. Thus, we often know that these techniques have short-term benefits, but can only speculate about their long-term effects.

It is likely that different techniques will be effective for different types of racial and ethnic groups. Students' cognitive, social, and emotional development also need to be taken into consideration when selecting techniques to improve intergroup relations. For instance, techniques that rely on empathic abilities cannot be used effectively until children have developed role-taking skills; the use of tasks that require abstract reasoning skills must await the emergence of such skills; and techniques that touch on emotion-laden experiences require that students have reached some level of emotional maturity. However, techniques that rely on cooperative social interaction in semistructured settings can be implemented with young as well as older students. And children can be taught about the customs, practices, and cultures of different groups from an early age, although some techniques are best reserved for older students. A great deal of additional research must be done before we know the optimal ages at which to employ different techniques. Until more research has been done, teachers will have to rely on their own best judgments concerning which techniques are likely to be most effective with their particular students. I suggest that as you read the recommendations, you think about the circumstances in which you might apply them and consider what modifications might be needed to use them effectively in that context.

In making the following recommendations, I focus primarily on the underlying rationale, although I will mention some of the techniques that have been used to implement them, when this information is available.

RECOMMENDATIONS RELATING TO SOCIAL INFORMATION PROCESSING

In this section I offer a variety of suggestions regarding problems that arise because of the biases that occur when students process information about other groups. Specifically, I will make recommendations concerning categorization, ingroup/outgroup evaluative biases, biased labeling, group differences and similarities, stereotyping, self-fulfilling prophecies, empathy, and positive versus negative emotions.

Social Categories

Intergroup relations programs can teach students about the nature of social categories and the consequences of categorization. Categorization is a natural part of social information processing, but research indicates that the mere act of categorizing people into ingroup and outgroup members can result in prejudice and discrimination (Tajfel, 1981; Tajfel & Turner, 1986). Students commonly categorize others in terms of attributes that are readily available in social interaction situations, such as race, ethnicity, gender, age, disabilities, and social class (McArthur, 1982; Stangor, Lynch, Duan, & Glass, 1992). Students use these categories because they seem to facilitate interaction by providing expectancies concerning the values, norms, and behavior of others. Making distinctions between groups often leads to both the perception that the outgroup is more uniform than the ingroup and an exaggeration of the differences between the groups (Linville, 1982; Linville, Salovey, & Fischer, 1986; Quattrone, 1986; Tajfel & Turner, 1986). As a result of these biases, rigid expectancies and behaviors based on them become the foundation for relations with outgroup members.

Intergroup contact can help ingroup members to see outgroup

members as individuals if the situation allows members of each group to behave in differing ways across a variety of contexts so their full humanity and diversity are displayed. A similar goal can be achieved in noncontact situations by providing ingroup members with information about multiple outgroup members who behave in diverse ways across a variety of situations (Crocker et al., 1983; Johnston & Hewstone, 1992; Mackie et al., 1992; Rothbart & John, 1985).

Experiential exercises also can be used to teach students about these fundamental aspects of categorization. One such technique involves a simulation that uses a separation of students by eye color to demonstrate the arbitrariness of intergroup distinctions and discrimination. On the first day of this simulation the brown-eyed children are encouraged to consider themselves as the more privileged group and they are allowed to treat the blue-eyed children as inferior. On the second day, the roles are reversed. One study using this technique found that it increased the participants' intentions to act in nondiscriminatory ways (Byrnes & Kiger, 1990).

Another approach to modifying categorization processes involves cognitive skills training (Aboud, 1998). In one study, fifth-grade students were provided with materials from *More than Meets the Eye* (Bowers & Swanson, 1988) for two classes a week for 11 weeks. The primary theme that runs through these materials is that internal qualities of individuals are more important than the external features of race. The goal of the program is to help students "process individualized information about peers from different racial and ethnic groups" (Aboud, 1998, p. 9). A carefully conducted evaluation of this curriculum found that it decreased the prejudices of the most high-prejudiced White students.

Personalizing Outgroup Members

Relations between students from different groups will improve if students learn to treat other people as individuals who are judged on their own merits, not on the basis of the groups to which they belong (except when the others wish to be treated in terms of these group memberships). Research suggests that individualizing or personalizing members of outgroups not only improves relations with these particular people, but also may reduce prejudice toward the groups to which they belong (Brewer & Miller, 1984; Miller & Harrington, 1990). Personalization also releases outgroup members from some of the burdens imposed on them by stereotyping. To implement this recommendation, mixed cooperative groups can be arranged is such a way that group membership is de-emphasized and the personal characteristics of the participants are emphasized (Bettencourt et al., 1992; Miller & Harrington, 1990). In general, students from different groups will benefit most from interacting with one another in situations in which they can get to know one another as individuals—the kinds of situations in which friendships can develop.

Biased Perceptions

Students also will benefit from learning about the biases that lead to perceptions of the ingroup as predominantly positive and the outgroup as predominantly negative. Social identities (identifications with the groups to which we belong) are important components of overall self-identity. One way that students can maintain positive self-esteem is to enhance their social identities by favorably evaluating the groups to which they belong (Tajfel & Turner, 1986). Although feeling positively about the ingroup can increase self-esteem, it often does so at the cost of negatively evaluating outgroups. Another way in which ingroup members maintain favorable impressions of their group is by giving biased explanations for the behaviors of ingroup and outgroup members (Hewstone, 1990; Hewstone & Jaspars, 1982; Pettigrew, 1979b). Ingroup members are given credit for the positive things they do, while outgroup members are blamed for negative behaviors or outcomes.

These "blaming the outgroup" responses could be reduced if students were helped to understand the seemingly automatic biases that lead to these distorted perceptions. They could be taught not only how such biases serve to enhance the ingroup at the expense of the outgroup, but also how the outgroup is subject to the same biases, leading almost inevitably to differences in perceptions. Schaller and colleagues (1996) have taught college students to overcome biases in intergroup perceptions caused by illogical reasoning. Students have a tendency to not take into consideration factors that may be the real causes of differences between groups and instead ascribe group differences to negative traits possessed by outgroup members. Students can learn to form accurate impressions of groups if they are trained to do so. For instance, as part of the training, students were asked if they would believe a person who claimed to be a better tennis player than the current no. 1 ranked player in the world because he had won all of his matches this year, while the no. 1 ranked player had lost some matches. It is likely that younger students, too, can be taught to overcome biases created by the motivation to perceive the ingroup in a favorable light.

Biased Labeling

Intergroup relations programs can present students with information about outgroups that challenges their negative evaluations of traits that the outgroup actually possesses. Some stereotyped traits refer to real differences between the groups that both the ingroup and the outgroup acknowledge. For instance, people with different national backgrounds (e.g., immigrant groups), ethnic groups, and religious groups do have different customs, norms, and values. The question is how such real differences should be presented. The problem that often arises is that, while the ingroup and the outgroup both acknowledge that the outgroup possesses a given trait, the ingroup evaluates the trait negatively, whereas the outgroup evaluates it positively. For instance, Asian-Americans are perceived to be high achievers, but this seemingly positive trait often is viewed negatively by members of other groups. Asian-Americans may be seen by non-Asian-Americans as overachievers, obsessed with getting ahead, or driven to achieve. To give another example, Jones (1991, 1997) argues that African-Americans have a different sense of time than do Whites, and that Whites evaluate this difference negatively. Jones traces the African-American sense of time to African cultures in which there was more emphasis on the present and the past than on the future, and in which time was tied to naturally occurring events (e.g., day and night, the seasons). In contrast, Whites' sense of time derives from Western cultures in which time is treated as a commodity that can be saved, used wisely, or wasted, and in which the future is more important than the present or the past.

What needs to be changed in these cases is the evaluation of the trait or the label applied to the trait. For instance, students can be told that loyalty to the ingroup is characteristic of all groups and does not represent clannishness in an outgroup any more than it does in the ingroup. Students can be shown that the negative traits they attribute to outgroups may be thought of in different ways—the outgroup is not stingy but thrifty, not pushy but assertive, not insincere but tactful, not conceited but confident, not snobbish but reserved, not religious fanatics but devoutly religious. The solution in these cases is not to provide information that disconfirms the stereotype, but to help students become aware of the tendency to label outgroup behaviors negatively. Students need to learn that just because outgroup members behave differently from the ingroup, that does not make their behavior wrong or bad. One way to present these contrasting differences is to put a list of negative traits on the board and then ask students what words can be used to transform the trait label to a positive one (e.g., lazy–easygoing, driven–hardworking, nosy–curious, insincere–tactful, wishy-washy–flexible).

Subjective Culture

Teachers also can help students to become knowledgeable about non-obvious, but real, group differences so that the students can come to accept and respect these differences. Some information concerning group differences needs to be explicitly taught because the differences are unlikely to be recognized, even though they may be creating discomfort, disruptions, or conflict. Many group differences are subtle, such as differences in nonverbal behavior and the implicit values that cultural and subcultural groups incorporate into their worldviews (Triandis, 1975, 1994). In addition to being unaware of the implicit values of other groups (the other groups' subjective culture), students are often unaware of their own values because so many values are inculcated at an age when there is no recognition that values are being acquired. Thus, students may find it worthwhile to learn about the implicit values of their own group, as well as the values of other groups.

Intercultural training programs indicate that it is possible to teach such differences using discussion and social interaction exercises, as well as more traditional classroom teaching methods (Black & Mendenhall, 1990). One such program demonstrated that training Whites to understand the subjective culture of African-Americans led to reductions in stereotyping (Weldon, Carlston, Rissman, Slobodin, & Triandis, 1975). The goal of this program was for the ingroup to be able to explain the behavior of members of the other group in terms of their "culture," not just to be able to acknowledge the existence of group differences. Particular practices of outgroup members may be rejected by the ingroup, unless the ingroup members understand the cultural context in which those practices are embedded. These practices may concern such important issues as the rituals associated with religion, but they just as easily can concern the meaning of silence in different groups, how loudly one speaks in public, or when it is permissible to ask personal questions. One technique that has been used to teach such information consists of programmed learning materials in which students answer multiple choice questions about misunderstandings and conflicts between groups and are given feedback on their answers (Cushner & Brislin, 1996).

Group Similarities

The similarities among the various racial and ethnic groups probably should receive special attention in intergroup relations programs. One of the best established findings in the social psychological literature is that similarity leads to liking (Byrne, 1971). Intergroup contact programs and intergroup training programs can capitalize on this important finding by ensuring that group similarities in values, norms, personality, standards, emotions, and behaviors are an explicit part of such programs. Emphasizing similarities is likely to make whatever differences exist more acceptable. In addition to whatever similarities may exist between any particular pair of groups in values, norms, and beliefs, the similarities among all groups based on universal needs for safety, belonging and love, self-esteem, and self-actualization (Maslow, 1970) also can be highlighted. As Allport (1954) noted, contact situations should emphasize the common humanity we all share.

Stereotype-Based Expectancies

It would be valuable for students to understand the mechanics of the stereotyping process, particularly the ways in which stereotype-based expectancies influence their behavior. Stereotypes are difficult to change because they are supported by self-perpetuating cognitive biases and behavioral tendencies. Although students often search for information about other groups in an unbiased manner (Devine, Hirt, & Gehrke, 1990), they easily can fall prey to a bias that leads them to seek out information that confirms their preconceptions (Johnston, 1996; Snyder, 1984). In addition, students tend to pay attention to, and process, stereotype-confirming information more easily than disconfirming evidence, unless the disconfirming evidence is especially strong and unambiguous (Hamilton et al., 1990; Srull et al., 1985). Even when stereotype-disconfirming evidence is processed, it is unlikely to change the stereotype because it often is explained away by attributing it to external, situational factors (Crocker et al., 1983). For instance, students often will attribute the success of an outgroup member to luck rather than skill. In addition, people often dislike others who fail to live up to their expectations (Costrich et al., 1975). To counteract the tendency to perceive that stereotypes have been confirmed, situations are needed in which stereotype disconfirmations are clear, occur frequently, are dispersed across a number of different members of the outgroup, and continue over time. To alter specific negative stereotypes, such as the view that members of the outgroup are unfriendly, teachers can create intergroup tasks that will lead members of the out-group to behave in friendly ways across a variety of situations.

Students often base their behaviors on their stereotypes, which can increase the chances that outgroup members will respond by fulfilling the ingroup members' expectations (Snyder, 1992). To help students to counteract the effects of their stereotypes on their behavior, students need to learn to recognize their own stereotypes. This idea derives from social compunction theory (Devine, 1989), which suggests that most members of our society have been exposed to the prevailing negative stereotypes of racial and ethnic outgroups during their socialization. Even individuals who wish not to be prejudiced are usually conversant with these stereotypes. Unfortunately, these early learned stereotypes can be activated automatically in social situations and can affect behavior unless their influence is consciously overcome.

When students are made aware of the pernicious effects of stereotyping, it helps them to put into effect self-regulatory processes in which expressions of stereotypes evoke guilt. In students who are motivated to overcome stereotyping and prejudice, these guilt feelings will lead to the suppression of stereotype-related behaviors (Monteith, 1993). The idea here is to promote internally experienced feelings of discomfort (e.g., guilt) as a response to the activation of stereotypes (Monteith, Zuwerink, & Devine, 1994). Students also can be taught to counteract their stereotypes when they have been activated. One way to achieve this goal would be to remind students of the value they place on being nonprejudiced, fair, tolerant, and egalitarian. Research suggests that it may be useful to confront students with the discrepancies between their deeply held egalitarian values and the negative stereotypes and prejudices they may have acquired unintentionally while growing up (Rokeach, 1971).

It should be noted that there may be some danger in openly discussing stereotypes because such discussions may serve to introduce racial and ethnic stereotypes to students who are unaware of them or to reinforce them in students who already possess them. To reduce this possibility one could precede attempts to deal with the content of stereotypes with an exploration of the harmful effects of stereotyping, highlighting the painful aspects of being on the receiving end of stereotypes. For instance, in one study small mixed groups of employees in a factory with a multiracial workforce discussed their experiences of what it felt like to be stereotyped (Kamfer & Venter, 1994).

Self-fulfilling prophecies also can be undercut by having students interact with outgroup members in one-on-one situations where they have an opportunity to learn about each other. The research suggests that stereotypes are most likely to be put to rest if the students are encouraged to get the other person to like them and to try to form an accurate impression of the other person (which leads to nonstereotype-based information processing) (Neuberg, 1996; Neuberg et al., 1993). For instance, the students could be given a list of topics to use in interviews of one another. It is important that these situations be sufficiently structured so that they are not stressful or unpleasant. This type of exercise might be effective at the beginning of the school year, but it also can be used as an ice-breaker when cooperative learning groups are being created. The students who have interviewed each other can introduce their partners to the other members of the cooperative groups.

Superordinate Categories

Reminding students of the overarching categories that unite them can be an effective way of reducing intergroup tensions. In one of the classic studies of intergroup relations, Sherif and colleagues (1961) found that creating superordinate groups (i.e., groups that included all of the participants) improved relations between contending groups of children attending a summer camp. Similarly, research by Gaertner and his colleagues (Gaertner et al., 1989) has demonstrated that creating superordinate groups in laboratory settings improves intergroup relations. When membership in superordinate groups is salient, subgroup differences fade in importance. Creating cohesive superordinate groups increases liking among the group members, which can undercut previous animosities between the subgroups. In school settings, some of the superordinate groups that can be invoked and reinforced are the classroom, the grade, the school itself, the community, the state, the nation, and humankind. Also, role labels such as "student" or "athlete" can be used to unite students. The most immediate superordinate groups are likely to be the most impactful (e.g., students, young people, ninth graders), but identification with any superordinate groups potentially can offset prejudice between subgroups. For example, one way to get students to focus on their common humanity is to engage them in a discussion of the most important global environmental issues facing the peoples of the earth (e.g., pollution, destruction of the rain forests, global warming, the extinction of species). Similar discussions focusing on specific community or school problems also could be used to unite students.

Cross-Cutting Categories

It also would be valuable if students learned to recognize that every person is simultaneously a member of many social categories and that their own social categories overlap with those of many others and unite them with those others. Not only are students members of racial and ethnic groups, but they are simultaneously males or females, Protestants, Catholics, Jews, or Muslims, blue-eyed or brown-eyed, first-borns or later-borns, right-handed or left-handed, and so on. Research suggests that reminding people of the cross-cutting groups to which they belong can reduce prejudice (Commins & Lockwood, 1978; Hewstone, Islam, & Judd, 1993; Vanbeselaere, 1991). Thomson (1992) lists a variety of exercises that can be used to bring out cross-cutting categories. In one exercise she uses graphs and then groups and regroups students by asking questions such as, "Who has brothers in this school?", "Who has sisters in this school?", "What is your favorite sport?", "Whose first name begins with each letter of the alphabet?" The students place their names on each of the relevant graphs in the appropriate place.

Empathy

Intergroup tensions almost certainly would be relieved if students could learn to see the world from the perspective of other groups and to be sensitive to the suffering other groups have experienced historically. This is especially true for the suffering of minority groups, but it also applies to understanding components of the majority group (e.g., European ethnic groups, such as the Irish). Multicultural education provides such information, as do other history-based approaches to teaching ethnic diversity (Banks, 1987, 1988, 1991; Fine, 1993; Ramsey, 1987). Being able to view the members of other groups within the context of their histories should foster both an understanding of, and a tolerance for, group differences.

In addition to learning about the history of discrimination, students can be taught about the current suffering of racial, ethnic, and religious groups due to prejudice, stereotyping, and discrimination. Laboratory research has demonstrated that encouraging White students to empathize with the everyday experiences of prejudice and stereotyping suffered by African-Americans can lead to reductions in stereotyping and more positive attitudes toward African-Americans (Finlay & Stephan, 1997). Role-taking exercises also have been found to increase empathy for outgroups and thereby improve intergroup relations (McGregor, 1993; Smith, 1990). Perceiving the suffering of others as if it were one's

own makes it more difficult to maintain negative stereotypes and attitudes toward outgroups (McGregor, 1993). However, McGregor (1993)
warns that classroom activities illustrating the existence of racism and
discrimination may be perceived as threatening by members of the
groups that have been discriminated against and by members of groups
that have engaged in discrimination. For this reason, and also because
older children have better developed empathic skills, it is probably better to use empathy exercises with older, rather than younger, students.
These age restrictions do not apply to the use of mixed cooperative
learning groups, which also have been found to increase empathy for
members of other groups, even in primary school students (Aronson &
Bridgeman, 1979; Bridgeman, 1977).

Positive Moods and Outcomes

It is important to create intergroup contact situations that elicit positive emotions, rather than negative ones (Fein & Spencer, 1997; Wilder & Simon, 1996). Cognitions of social groups are associated with
positive and negative emotions (Fiske & Pavelchak, 1986; Stephan &
Stephan, 1993). Outgroups are all too commonly associated with negative emotions such as fear, anger, disgust, resentment, and hatred. To
dilute the impact of the negative emotions linked to outgroups, positive
emotions need to be linked to outgroups as well. These linkages can be
created by associating outgroup members with positive experiences.
Athletics and other cooperative extracurricular activities can work toward this goal, as can the use of cooperative groups in classroom settings (Johnson & Johnson, 1992a). It is important that every effort be
made to promote positive outcomes and positive emotions in such settings. Competition between members of different groups can have a
corrosive effect on intergroup relations because it frequently engenders
hostility and negative social comparisons.

The two most powerful techniques to reverse the information processing biases I have just reviewed are the use of mixed cooperative
learning groups and multicultural education (Aronson et al., 1978; Aronson & Patnoe, 1997; Banks, 1987, 1988, 1994, 1997; Cohen, 1986; Johnson & Johnson, 1992a; Johnson, Johnson, & Holubec, 1994; Slavin, 1992;
Stahl, 1994). There is no reason why the two techniques could not be
combined. That is, the material that students in cooperative groups
would be teaching each other would be multicultural curriculum mod-
ules. Cooperative learning groups contain all of the elements thought
to be important for beneficial intergroup contact. The interaction in
such groups is cooperative, individualized, equal status, and supported

by authority figures. The interactions in these groups, combined with the use of multicultural materials, would provide students with information about outgroup members that disconfirmed their stereotypes.

Cooperative groups studying multicultural materials would increase the students' ability to take the role of outgroup members, as well as provide them with information about shared values. These groups also would enable students to learn how to interact with outgroup members in a situation that is relatively nonthreatening. The cohesion of cooperative groups should increase liking for group members, some of whom are from racial, ethnic, or religious outgroups. This liking for individual outgroup members is likely to generalize to the outgroup as a whole if students have an opportunity to interact with a number of different outgroup members. Generalization of favorable attitudes also could be furthered by assigning students to groups in ways that do not increase the salience of race or ethnicity and by including exercises that are interpersonally oriented (e.g., interviewing one another, role playing, learning to paraphrase), rather than having the groups be exclusively task-oriented. Efforts also should be made to encourage positive interactions that lead to successful outcomes in cooperative learning groups to capitalize on the effects of positive moods and avoid the problems associated with failure and negative moods. Finally, cooperative learning groups have the added benefit of increasing the self-esteem and achievement of minority students, without decreasing the achievement of majority group students.

RECOMMENDATIONS RELATING TO VALUE AND IDENTITY ISSUES

The next section contains suggestions regarding values that are relevant to improving intergroup relations. The particular values discussed are egalitarianism, universal values, American values, and diversity. The section also contains suggestions for techniques of strengthening and affirming ingroup identity without simultaneously creating problems in intergroup relations.

Egalitarianism

The value of egalitarianism can be emphasized and reinforced in the classroom. Equal status was one of the basic components of the original contact hypothesis, as formulated by Allport (1954). Allport argued that contact under equal-status conditions would dispel prejudice and instill notions of equality between groups. Theories of modern racism that address the complexity of intergroup attitudes in the late twentieth century acknowledge the existence of feelings or beliefs that promote racism, but they also specify a countervailing force, usually egalitarianism, that restricts direct expressions of prejudice (Gaertner & Dovidio, 1986; Katz, Glass, & Wackenhut, 1986). Augmenting the strength of these egalitarian sentiments should reduce prejudice and stereotyping.

The lesson that Myrdal (1944) taught us in *An American Dilemma* is still worth teaching—there continues to be a contradiction between the inequalities in our society and our democratic values of equality and freedom. To comprehend this contradiction, students can be taught how the groups in power use legitimizing myths (e.g., the innate inferiority of minority groups) to justify the hierarchical systems from which they benefit (Sidanius, 1993; Sidanius & Pratto, 1993). Teachers can help students to understand the system of power and prestige that created and maintains ethnic, race, gender, religious, and social class hierarchies. It also would be valuable for students to learn how the political, economic, and social inequalities that exist in our society affect the lives of its people (Nieto, 1995). Adopting this suggestion means selecting materials for history and social studies courses that present a more critical perspective on the origins and nature of the social structure of our society than commonly is presented in most classroom materials. The rationale behind this suggestion is that if students are to learn how to overcome prejudice and stereotyping in their own lives and in society, it may be necessary to openly examine racism and other components of social systems that provide privileges to some groups over others, rather than avoiding these issues because it is uncomfortable to deal with them. This recommendation probably cannot be implemented with younger students. A study of university students taking an intergroup relations course based on intergroup contact, active exercises, and lectures found that these students were better able to understand the structural causes of racial/ethnic inequalities after the course than was a control group (Lopez, Gurin, & Nagda, 1998).

Cohen (1984, 1986; Cohen & Roper, 1972; Cohen et al., 1994) uses multiracial cooperative groups to produce equality of treatment between groups. In order to counteract negative stereotypes of minority groups, she creates tasks that allow all of the group members to display abilities at which they excel. Other cooperative techniques have attempted to promote equality in cooperative intergroup contact situations by assigning the participants roles of equal importance or rotating the more important roles (e.g., teacher, learner) (Aronson et al., 1978; Aronson & Patnoe, 1997).

Universalistic Values

In addition to emphasizing egalitarianism, teachers could stress the importance of other universalistic values such as justice, fairness, dignity, respect, peace, compassion, and charity. Universalistic values are part of the common humanity that all peoples and all religions share (Kohlberg, 1981; Schwartz, 1992; Schwartz & Bilsky, 1990). These universalistic values are in direct opposition to prejudice, stereotyping, and discrimination, so promoting these values tends to directly undermine racial injustice and unfair treatment of outgroup members. In their discussions of moral development programs for elementary students, Davidson and Davidson (1994) and Akin (1995) offer a number of suggestions for techniques (stories, discussions, role plays) that could be applied to the teaching of universal values. A consideration of universalistic values could supplement the more narrowly focused moral education programs that are designed primarily to help students learn to make conscious decisions about what is right and wrong.

American Values

There is a widespread consensus in American society concerning many other values, including the importance of education, freedom, the value of rationality (analytical reasoning, logic), the importance of family, the utility of science and technology, the benefits of democracy, the need to safeguard basic human rights, and the importance of maintaining good health. Thus, there are many values that unite the different racial, ethnic, and religious groups in America. These values can be used to create a sense of common destiny and a feeling of kinship. Students would benefit from learning these values and how to put them in practice. The "Facing History" curriculum uses the experience of the Holocaust to raise many of these issues (Fine, 1993). Small group or class discussion of children's rights (Genser, 1985) also could be used as a starting point for wider-ranging discussions of the values Americans share. Banks and Clegg (1990) have developed techniques that help students to understand their values and make reflective choices. They employ moral dilemmas to aid students in recognizing value-relevant behavior, analyzing conflicting values, and examining behavioral consequences of values.

Diversity

Students also can be taught to place a positive value on diversity. Our strength as a nation has always come, to a considerable extent, from our diversity. Different groups with their different histories and tradi-tions have combined their ideas and talents in creative ways that have made us a world leader in technology, science, medicine, and industry. Students need to learn that because students from other groups have different worldviews and "cultures," they can offer different perspec-tives on solving problems that lead to better solutions. Having students work together on complex problems that demand a wide range of skills and knowledge can help them to learn the value of diversity (Cohen, 1986).

Racial, Ethnic, and Religious Identities

Teachers are in a position to assist students in learning to value their racial, ethnic, and religious identities. To accomplish this goal, students can be taught about the nature of identity in general, and racial, ethnic, and religious identity in particular, in ways that affirm these identities. Research suggests that students who are secure in their own group identities are less likely to discriminate against outgroups or openly express their prejudices and stereotypes (Aboud & Doyle, 1993; Gonza-les & Cauce, 1995). Thus, it should be possible to create strong ingroup identities without damaging intergroup relations. Teachers also can help students to feel pride in their group memberships and can instill self-respect in students about their group memberships by showing that they value the groups and by being fair, trustworthy, neutral, and respectful in their treatment of racial, ethnic, and other groups (Tyler et al., 1996).

However, there is some risk that creating positive ingroup identities will lead to rejection of outgroups. One solution to this problem would be to present group differences in such a way that they represent alter-native solutions to the problems of cultural life. Students could be taught that there are many valid ways of addressing the same human needs and problems (e.g., dealing with pain, suffering, and death; social-izing children; maintaining social control; creating belief systems, and so on). A multicultural curriculum that stresses the value of all groups by exploring their history and cultures is one technique that should promote secure ingroup identities without fostering negative views of other groups (Banks, 1987, 1988, 1994, 1997).

Strong ingroup identities carry with them the seeds of another po-tential problem. When strong ingroup identities are threatened, preju-dice easily can result (Branscombe & Wann, 1994). For this reason, it is particularly important to avoid presenting information on group differ-ences in a manner that the groups perceive as threatening.

RECOMMENDATIONS RELATING TO INTERGROUP RELATIONS SKILLS

The suggestions in this section are concerned with skills that would be useful when students are interacting with other students in intergroup settings. Among the sets of skills discussed are the ability to interact with outgroup members, resolve conflicts, and respond effectively to injustice.

Intergroup Interaction Skills

Intergroup relations programs can equip students with knowledge and social skills that will enable them to more effectively interact with people who are different from them. It seems reasonable to make an analogy here between international relations and domestic intergroup relations. That is, students in our society can be taught to interact more effectively across group lines by training them in some of the skills that have been found to be useful in cross-national relations (Bochner, 1986, 1993; Collett, 1971; Cupach & Canary, 1997). Some of the skills that have been found to be effective in cross-national interactions are being able to recognize and interpret differences in nonverbal behavior, making adjustments to others' behavior, tolerating ambiguity, avoiding the use of negative traits to explain the behavior of others, listening and observing carefully, asking questions when appropriate, paraphrasing others' comments to ensure understanding, taking the roles of people from other groups, being nonjudgmental, and being tolerant. These skills often are taught using role-playing exercises or group discussions of vignettes in which people who do not display these skills run into difficulties (the students could be asked to diagnose the problem and recommend solutions). These skills also can be taught in small groups (Roy, 1994).

In addition, intergroup relations programs can help students to learn how to feel comfortable when interacting with outgroup members. One of the primary causes of prejudice is fear. Students fear not only physical aggression, but also that members of other groups will reject them, take advantage of them, or simply behave in unpredictable ways. Fear leads members of social groups to avoid interacting with outgroup members and causes them discomfort when they do interact with outgroup members (Stephan & Stephan, 1996a). Fear and the discomfort it creates can undermine natural and effective social interaction and foster stereotyping and prejudice. To reduce anxiety and uncertainty concerning interaction with outgroup members, the contexts in which interaction takes place should be relatively structured, the balance of members of the different groups should be as equal as possible, the chances of failure or other negative outcomes such as rejection should be low, and opportunities for hostility and aggression should be minimized (Stephan & Stephan, 1985). In designing intergroup interaction situations, it might be useful to rely on relatively structured activities during the initial phases and then move on to less structured activities after the students are more at ease with one another.

A number of theories of prejudice emphasize the important role played by specific types of threats (Esses et al., 1993a; Gaertner & Dovidio, 1986; Katz, Glass, & Wackenhut, 1986; McConahay, 1986; Sears, 1988; Stephan & Stephan, 1996b). In the context of the larger society, these feelings of threat revolve around the possibility that the ingroup will lose some or all of its power or resources (realistic threats) or that its very way of life will be undermined (symbolic threats). Many of these fears have little basis in reality or are greatly exaggerated. Providing factual information that contradicts these misperceptions can counteract prejudices based on these false threats. Stressing the value similarities that exist between groups should reduce the degree of symbolic threats posed by outgroups and thus reduce fear and prejudice. In the school context, realistic threats arise in disputes over power, status, territory, and control of valued resources, while symbolic threats center on the dominance of the norms, values, interests, and preferences (music, dress, language) of one group over another. These threats can be mitigated by the evenhanded treatment of all groups by teachers and administrators. It also might be useful to have students discuss their fears in class discussions and then have them suggest ways of lessening the fears, while at the same time exposing how unrealistic some of the perceived threats are.

Conflict Resolution Skills

Relations between groups are likely to improve if students are taught about the origins of intergroup conflict and techniques of resolving conflict, because an important part of learning to solve conflicts is understanding their origins. Intergroup conflict originates not only in disputes over real resources (e.g., power, turf, money) and differences in values, beliefs, and norms, but also in the failure of one group to meet another group's needs for respect, affirmation, or acceptance. Research indicates that students can be trained to mediate conflicts that arise in schools (Deutsch, 1993; Johnson & Johnson, 1995a, 1995b; Johnson et al., 1995). Students also can be taught how to avoid conflicts by learning about techniques of de-escalation, such as negotiation, bargaining, making concessions, or giving apologies or explanations (Fisher, 1990, 1994; Palomares, Logan, Weber, Willson, & Kellison, 1975). Multiracial and multiethnic schools probably would benefit from creating formal mechanisms to resolve intergroup disputes, such as dispute resolution centers that employ student mediators under the direction of faculty members (Johnson & Johnson, 1995a, 1995b; Looking for America, 1994). If there are ongoing ethnic, racial, or religious conflicts in the school, another approach that might be useful would be to use conflict resolution workshops that bring together student leaders from the relevant groups to discuss the conflicts under the direction of a facilitator (Kelman, 1990; Kelman & Cohen, 1986). The dispute resolution centers that offer free services in so many communities around the country could be a valuable resource in providing training and volunteers.

Intergroup relations also will benefit if students learn how to perceive, understand, and respond to group differences in behavior. In particular, students need to learn how to avoid offending members of other groups. They should also know how to avoid responding as if they had been offended when no offense was intended (e.g., when members of the outgroup behave in unexpected ways). Students could be taught these lessons through the use of vignettes portraying situations in which members of one group unintentionally offend another group and the receiving group responds negatively to the offense. In a contrasting set of vignettes the receiving group could realize the offense was unintentional and not respond as if they had been offended. Students could discuss these contrasting vignettes in small groups. Friction between members of different groups could be reduced if students realized that when outgroup members behave in ways that are inconsistent with the norms of their own group, it does not necessarily mean that members of the other group are behaving antagonistically. For instance, when Native-Americans from the Southwest remain silent while members of other groups are engaged in social interaction, no disrespect is intended toward the members of the other groups (Basso, 1990).

Responding to Injustice

Students may find it valuable to know how to respond when they see injustices taking place. They can be taught about the remedies for discrimination, prejudice, and stereotyping that are available to them in their own schools. Students are going to witness discrimination, prejudice, and stereotyping and they should to be equipped with the skills to deal with these situations effectively. Responding effectively means knowing about the school codes for hate speech, acts of discrimination, sexual harassment, and related issues. Awareness of the remedies provides students with a means of reacting to these problems when they arise and informs them of the consequences, should they engage in such acts.

In addition, it would be valuable to provide students with the means to respond informally to the racist and sexist comments and "jokes" that occur in everyday interaction, but are not subject to formal sanctions. The responses will depend on the context in which these problems arise, but there are circumstances in which disapproval of these acts can be expressed effectively. In their group training sessions for employees of large corporations in South Africa, Kamfer and Venter (1994) used discussion in mixed-race groups to bring out possible responses to acts of everyday racism and sexism (cf. Katz & Ivey, 1977). It should be possible to hold similar discussions in school settings.

Students definitely would benefit from learning how to react constructively when they themselves are the targets of stereotyping, prejudice, and discrimination. Being the target of stereotyping, prejudice, and discrimination is a painful experience. People react in a variety of different ways, many of them potentially damaging. For instance, some people respond with anger, rage, and violence, while others reciprocate the prejudice and discrimination. There are also individuals who react by accepting the stereotypes as potentially applicable to themselves or by becoming depressed and feeling helpless. Students will be better off if they learn a range of coping responses and ways of avoiding potentially dysfunctional responses directed at the perpetrators or themselves. Filing grievances, protests using legitimate means, social disapproval of perpetrators, sanctions against perpetrators, changes in policies, negotiation with offending groups or individuals, and using mediators are among the potential responses that may be effective.

In addition, it would be useful for students to learn how to separate negative feedback based on group membership from that based on their personal behavior. Students who are the targets of prejudice and stereotyping can be made aware of the pitfalls of explaining all criticism and negative reactions from outgroup members in terms of prejudice. This attribution limits their capacity to learn from real mistakes they have made that actually merited negative feedback (Crocker & Major, 1989).

RECOMMENDATIONS RELATING TO THE SOCIAL CULTURE
OF THE SCHOOLS

In this final section I will make a series of suggestions for changing the social culture of the schools in ways that should facilitate positive relations between groups. The recommendations deal with modeling positive intergroup relations, creating incentives for nondiscriminatory behavior and sanctions for discriminatory behavior, and the need to train teachers in intergroup relations.

Organizational Culture

The organizational culture of the schools should reflect the desired relations between racial and ethnic groups. That is, relations among administrators, teachers, and support personnel should be a model for the types of intergroup relations students are expected to display. According to social learning theory, a great deal of human behavior is acquired through observation (Bandura, 1986). This recommendation capitalizes on the idea that nondiscriminatory behavior can be acquired through exposure to models who behave in nondiscriminatory ways. Research suggests that the most effective models are those who are respected by the observers (because they have high status, competence, or power), to whom the observers are attracted, and who find the behavior rewarding. Using these criteria, it is obvious that administrators and teachers are important models for the acquisition of intergroup relations skills and behaviors.

Intergroup relations programs are likely to be much more successful in a organizational climate that promotes positive intergroup relations among the administration, faculty, and staff than in one that does not. If basic democratic values of equality and participatory decision making are considered to be valuable for students, the adults in their environment must display these types of attitudes and behaviors toward one another. If intergroup collaboration is sought in students, the administrators, teachers, and staff should show the way. If students are expected to treat each other with civility, tolerance, and respect, then the administrators, faculty, and staff should model these behaviors. Similarly, the students' parents should be shown respect for their cultural and racial backgrounds. One of the basic tenets of the original contact hypothesis was that support by authority figures was essential to improve intergroup relations (Allport, 1954). Not only should school authorities support positive intergroup relations, but they need to model these behaviors in their own conduct. In addition, as Cohen and others (Cohen, 1980; Schofield, 1995) have suggested, the racial, ethnic, and gender composition of the administrative, teaching, and support staffs of schools sets the tone for interactions within the schools. It is important that the racial and ethnic groups represented among the students be well represented among the administrators, teachers, and support staff.

Codes of Conduct and Incentives

Schools can provide incentives for nondiscriminatory behavior. This recommendation is straightforward in rationale, but implementing it may require some creativity. The premise is simple: that rewarded behavior increases in frequency. In practice, this recommendation implies that the organizational culture and normative structure of the school explicitly promote positive intergroup relations. The idea is to undermine ethnocentrism and intergroup hostility by promoting civility, respect, and tolerance between groups. Multicultural curricula in which the history and culture of all groups are presented can help to create this type of climate, as can active exposure to the art, music, dance, food, and other cultural elements of all groups. It also may be helpful to train teachers to explicitly reinforce nondiscriminatory behaviors in their classrooms. In one study, students were rewarded for sitting next to students of another race at lunch (Hauserman, Walen, & Behling, 1973), which resulted in increased cross-racial interaction during and after the lunch period.

School policies should make it clear that overt stereotyping, prejudice, and discrimination will be met with social disapproval and sanctions. Strong codes of conduct should be established that punish intentional hate speech and overt acts of intergroup aggression. The basic human rights and obligations of all students should be delineated clearly. These policies could be developed by administrators and teachers, but they may be more effective if they are generated through consensus among the students, or through a congress of faculty, parents, community members, and students (Nieto, 1994).

Teacher Training

Teachers may need explicit training in the implementation of the types of recommendations being made here (Banks, 1997). Teachers are the key to improving intergroup relations in the schools, and many are ill-equipped to do so. As Slavin (1995) has noted, teachers need to be trained in intergroup relations as a part of their own education. They may need to learn not only about the cultures of the students they will teach, but also about specific techniques of improving intergroup relations in their classrooms. Training in intergroup relations skills should be a routine part of every teacher's training. Teachers also could be provided with inservice training to help them acquire these skills, and they should be encouraged and supported if they wish to take courses that will further equip them with these skills.

In ancient times, physicians were admonished to heal themselves. In a similar vein, teachers also must teach themselves. Nearly all of America's teachers were raised in this society, with its racial divisions and tragic history of genocide, slavery, internment, deportation, riots, and discrimination in employment, housing, education, and health care. Having been raised in this society has exposed us all to the legacy of this history. We must each look within ourselves to see if we hold unexamined stereotypes that are negative, overgeneralized, or irrational; if we enjoy being with some groups more than others; if we are more comfortable interacting with the members of one group than another; and if we see the values and practices of our own group not only as good for our group, but as somehow more proper, more natural, or better than those of other groups. We are all human, which means we are fallible and susceptible to biases of which we are unaware—biases that can affect our thinking and our actions. We can and should appreciate and value our personal histories, but we should not let them interfere with our ability to teach our students. We have an obligation to make every effort to overcome any limitations imposed us on by our histories and human frailty. Our students deserve nothing less.

RELATED SETS OF RECOMMENDATIONS

Hawley, W. D., Banks, J. A., Padilla, A. M., Pope-Davis, D. B., & Schofield, J. W. (1995). Strategies for reducing racial and ethnic prejudice: Essential principles for program design. In W. D. Hawley & A. W. Jackson (Eds.), *Toward a common destiny: Improving race and ethnic relations in America* (pp. 423–433). San Francisco: Jossey-Bass.

NCSS Task Force (1992, September). Curriculum guidelines for multicultural education. *Social Education*, pp. 274–294.

REFERENCES

Aboud, F. E. (1998). *Evaluation of a fifth grade program to reduce prejudice.* Unpublished manuscript, McGill University, Montreal.

Aboud, F. E., & Doyle, A. B. (1993). The early development of ethnic identity and attitudes. In M. E. Bernal & G. P. Knight (Eds.), *Ethnic identity: Formation and transmission among Hispanics and other minorities* (pp. 47–59). Albany: State University of New York Press.

Aboud, F. E., & Doyle, A. B. (1996). Does talk of race foster prejudice or tolerance in children? *Canadian Journal of Behavioral Science, 28,* 161–170.

Ackerman, N., & Jahoda, M. (1950). *Anti-Semitism and emotional disorders: A psycho-analytic interpretation.* New York: Harper.

Adlerfer, C. P. (1982). Problems of changing white males' behavior and beliefs concerning race relations. In P. Goodman & Associates (Eds.), *Change in organizations* (pp. 122–165). San Francisco: Jossey-Bass.

Akin, T. (1995). *Character education in America's schools.* Spring Valley, CA: Innerchoice.

Allen, V. L., & Wilder, D. A. (1975). Categorization, belief similarity, and group discrimination. *Journal of Personality and Social Psychology, 32,* 971–977.

Allport, F. H., et al. (1953). The effects of segregation and the consequences of desegregation: A social science statement. *Minnesota Law Review, 37,* 429–440.

Allport, G. W. (1954). *The nature of prejudice.* Reading, MA: Addison-Wesley.

Amir, Y. (1976). The role of intergroup contact in change of prejudice and race relations. In P. A. Katz (Ed.), *Towards the elimination of racism* (pp. 245–308). New York: Pergamon.

Andersen, S. M., & Klatzky, R. (1987). Traits and social stereotypes: Levels of categorization in person perception. *Journal of Personality and Social Psychology, 53,* 235–246.

Anderson, J. R. (1983). *The architecture of cognition.* Cambridge, MA: Harvard University Press.

Araki, C. (1990). Dispute management in the schools. *Mediation Quarterly, 8,* 51–62.

Armor, D. J. (1980). White flight and the future of desegregation. In W. G. Stephan & J. Feagin (Eds.), *School desegregation: Past, present, and future* (pp. 187–226). New York: Plenum.

Armor, D. J. (1988). School busing: A time for change. In P. A. Katz & D. A. Taylor (Eds.), *Eliminating racism: Profiles in controversy* (pp. 259–280). New York: Plenum.

Aronson, E., & Bridgeman, D. (1979). Jigsaw groups and the desegregated classroom: In pursuit of common goals. *Personality and Social Psychology Bulletin, 5,* 438–446.

Aronson, E., Blaney, N., Stephan, C., Sikes, J., & Snapp, M. (1978). *The jigsaw classroom.* Beverly Hills, CA: Sage.

Aronson, E., & Patnoe, S. (1997). *The jigsaw classroom.* New York: Longman.

Aronson, E., & Thibodeau, R. (1992). The jigsaw classroom: A cooperative strategy for reducing prejudice. In J. Lynch, C. Modgil, & S. Modgil (Eds.), *Cultural diversity in the schools* (Vol. II, pp. 231–256). London: Falmer Press.

Ashmore, R. D., & Del Boca, F. K. (1976). Psychological approaches to understanding intergroup conflict. In P. A. Katz (Ed.), *Towards the elimination of racism* (pp. 73–124). New York: Pergamon.

Astin, A. (1982). *Minorities in American education.* San Francisco: Jossey-Bass.

Bandura, A. (1986). *Social foundations of thought and action: A social cognitive theory.* Englewood Cliffs, NJ: Prentice-Hall.

Baker, S. M., & Devine, P. G. (1988, March). *Faces as primes for stereotype activation.* Paper presented as the Midwestern Psychological Association, Chicago.

Banaji, M. R., Hardin, C., & Rothman, A. J. (1993). Implicit stereotyping in person judgment. *Journal of Personality and Social Psychology, 65,* 272–281.

Banks, J. A. (1987). *Teaching strategies for ethnic studies* (4th ed.). Boston: Allyn & Bacon.

Banks, J. A. (1988). *Multicultural education* (2nd ed.). Boston: Allyn & Bacon.

Banks, J. A. (1991). *Teaching strategies for ethnic studies* (5th ed.). Boston: Allyn & Bacon.

Banks, J. A. (1994). *An introduction to multicultural education* (3rd ed.). Boston: Allyn & Bacon.

Banks, J. A. (1995a). Approaches to multicultural curriculum reform. In J. A. Banks & C. A. McGee Banks (Eds.), *Multicultural education: Issues and perspectives* (2nd ed.; pp. 195–214). Boston: Allyn & Bacon.

Banks, J. A. (1995b). Multicultural education and the modification of racial attitudes. In W. D. Hawley & A. W. Jackson (Eds.), *Toward a common destiny* (pp. 315–339). San Francisco: Jossey-Bass.

Banks, J. A. (1997). *Educating citizens in a multicultural society.* New York: Teachers College Press.

Banks, J. A., & Clegg, A. A. (1990). *Teaching strategies for social studies: Theory and practice* (4th ed.). White Plains, NY: Longman.

Bargh, J. A. (1984). Automatic and conscious processing of social information. In R. S. Wyer & T. K. Skrull (Eds.), *Handbook of social cognition* (pp. 1–44). Hillsdale, NJ: Erlbaum.

Bargh, J. A. (1988). Automatic information processing: Implications for communication and affect. In L. Donophew, H. E. Sypher & T. E. Higgins (Eds.),

Communication, social cognition and affect (pp. 9–32). Hillsdale, NJ: Erlbaum.

Basso, K. H. (1990). "To give up on words": Silence in Western Apache culture. In D. Carbaugh (Ed.), *Cultural communication and intercultural contact* (pp. 305–320). Hillsdale, NJ: Erlbaum.

Bettencourt, B. A., Brewer, M. B., Rogers-Croak, M., & Miller, N. (1992). Cooperation and the reduction of intergroup bias: The role of reward structure and social orientation. *Journal of Experimental Social Psychology, 28,* 301–319.

Bettencourt, B. A., Dill, K. E., Greathouse, S. A., Charlton, K., & Mulholland, A. (1997). Evaluations of ingroup and outgroup: The role of category-based expectancy violation. *Journal of Experimental Social Psychology, 33,* 244–275.

Bhawuk, D. P. S. (1990). Cross-cultural orientation programs. In R. W. Brislin (Ed.), *Applied cross-cultural psychology* (pp. 235–346). Newbury Park, CA: Sage.

Billig, M., & Tajfel, H. (1973). Social categorization and similarity in intergroup behavior. *European Journal of Social Psychology, 3,* 27–52.

Black, J. S., & Mendenhall, M. (1990). Cross-cultural training effectiveness: A review and theoretical framework for future research. *Academy of Management Review, 15,* 113–136.

Blanchard, F. A. (1992, May). Combatting intentional bigotry and inadvertently racist acts. *Chronicle of Higher Education,* p. 13.

Blanchard, F. A., Adelman, L., & Cook, S. W. (1975). Effect of group success and failure upon interpersonal attraction in cooperating interracial groups. *Journal of Personality and Social Psychology, 31,* 1020–1030.

Blanchard, F. A., & Cook, S. W. (1976). Effects of helping a less competent member of a cooperating interracial group on the development of interpersonal attraction. *Journal of Personality and Social Psychology, 34,* 1245–1255.

Blaney, N., Stephan, C., Rosenfield, D., Aronson, E., & Sikes, J. (1977). Interdependence in the classroom: A field study. *Journal of Educational Psychology, 69,* 121–128.

Blatt, M. M., & Kohlberg, L. (1975). The effects of classroom moral discussion on children's level of moral reasoning. *Journal of Moral Education, 4,* 129–161.

Blumberg, R. G., & Roye, W. J. (1980). *Interracial bonds.* New York: General Hall.

Bobo, L. (1988). Group conflict, prejudice, and the paradox of contemporary racial attitudes. In P. A. Katz & D. A. Taylor (Eds.), *Eliminating racism: Profiles in controversy* (pp. 85–116). New York: Plenum.

Bochner, S. (1982). The social psychology of cross-cultural relations. In S. Bochner (Ed.), *Cultures in contact* (pp. 5–44). New York: Pergamon.

Bochner, S. (1986). Training intercultural skills. In C. R. Hollins & P. Trower (Eds.), *Handbook of social skills training: Applications across the life span* (Vol. 1, pp. 155–184). Oxford: Pergamon.

Bochner, S. (1993). Culture shock. In W. Lonner & R. Malpass (Eds.), *Psychology and culture* (pp. 245–252). Boston: Allyn & Bacon.

Bodenhausen, G. V. (1988). Stereotypic biases in social decision making and memory: Testing process models for stereotype use. *Journal of Personality and Social Psychology, 55,* 726–737.

Bodenhausen, G. V. (1993). Emotions, arousal, and stereotype judgments: A heuristic model of affect and stereotyping. In D. M. Mackie & D. L. Hamilton (Eds.), *Affect, cognition, and stereotyping: Interactive processes in group perception* (pp. 13–37). San Diego: Academic Press.

Bodenhausen, G. V., Kramer, G. P., & Susser, K. (1993). *Happiness and stereotypic thinking in social judgment.* Unpublished manuscript, Michigan State University, East Lansing.

Bodenhausen, G. V., Sheppard, L. A., & Kramer, G. P. (1994). Negative affect and social judgment: The differential impact of anger and sadness. *European Journal of Social Psychology, 24,* 45–62.

Bodenhausen, G. V., & Wyer, R. S., Jr. (1985). Effects of stereotypes on decision making and information-processing strategies. *Journal of Personality and Social Psychology, 48,* 267–282.

Borgida, E., & Omoto, A. M. (1986, August). *Racial stereotyping and prejudice: The role of personal involvement.* Paper presented at the meeting of the American Psychological Association, Washington, DC.

Bovasso, G. (1993). Self, group, and public interests motivating racial politics. *Political Psychology, 14,* 3–20.

Bower, G. H. (1980). Mood and memory. *American Psychologist, 36,* 129–148.

Bowers, V., & Swanson, D. (1988). *More than meets the eye.* Vancouver: Pacific Educational Press.

Braddock, J. H., II (1987, March). *The impact of segregated school experiences on college and major field choices of black high school graduates: Evidence from the high school and beyond survey.* Paper presented at the National Conference on School Desegregation, Chicago.

Braddock, J. H., II, Crain, R., & McPartland, J. (1984). A long-term view of desegregation: Some recent studies of graduates as adults. *Phi Delta Kappan, 66,* 259–264.

Braddock, J. H., II, Dawkins, M. P., & Wilson, G. (1995). Intercultural contact and race relations among American youth. In W. D. Hawley & A. W. Jackson (Eds.), *Toward a common destiny* (pp. 237–256). San Francisco: Jossey-Bass.

Braddock, J. H., II, & McPartland, J. (1982). Assessing school desegregation effects: New directions in research. *Research in Sociology of Education and Socialization, 3,* 259–282.

Braddock, J. H., II, & McPartland, J. (1983). *More evidence on the social-psychological processes that perpetuate minority segregation: The relationship of school desegregation and employment desegregation.* Baltimore: Johns Hopkins University Press.

Braddock, J. H., II, & McPartland, J. (1987). How minorities continue to be excluded from equal employment opportunities: Research on labor market and institutional barriers. *Journal of Social Issues, 43,* 5–39.

Braddock, J. H., II, & McPartland, J. (1988, February). The social and academic consequences of school desegregation. *Equity and Choice,* pp. 5–10, 63–73.

Braddock, J. H., II, McPartland, J., & Trent, W. (1984, February). *Desegregated schools and desegregated work environments.* Paper presented at American Educational Research Association; San Francisco.

Braddock, J. H., II, & Slavin, R. E. (1993). Why ability grouping must end: Achieving excellence and equity in American education. *Journal of Intergroup Relations, 20,* 51–64.

Branscombe, N. R., & Wann, D. L. (1994). Collective self-esteem consequences of outgroup derogation when a valued social identity is on trial. *European Journal of Social Psychology, 24,* 641–657.

Breckheimer, S. E., & Nelson, R. O. (1976). Group methods for reducing racial prejudice and discrimination. *Psychological Reports, 39,* 1259–1268.

Brewer, M. B. (1979). In-group bias in the minimal intergroup situation: A cognitive-motivational analysis. *Psychological Bulletin, 86,* 307–324.

Brewer, M. B., & Miller, N. (1984). Beyond the contact hypothesis: Theoretical perspectives on desegregation. In N. Miller & M. B. Brewer (Eds.), *Groups in contact: The psychology of desegregation* (pp. 281–302). New York: Academic Press.

Brewer, M. B., & Miller, N. (1988). Contact and cooperation: When do they work? In P. A. Katz & D. A. Taylor (Eds.), *Eliminating racism: Profiles in controversy* (pp. 315–326). New York: Plenum.

Bridgeman, D. L. (1977). *The influence of cooperative interdependent learning on role taking and moral reasoning: A theoretical and empirical field study with fifth grade students.* Unpublished doctoral dissertation, University of California, Santa Cruz.

Brigham, J. C. (1971). Ethnic stereotypes. *Psychological Bulletin, 76,* 15–38.

Brigham, J. C. (1974). Views of black and white children concerning the distribution of personality characteristics. *Journal of Personality, 42,* 144–158.

Brislin, R. W., Cushner, K., Cherrie, C., & Yong, M. (1986). *Intercultural interactions: A practical guide.* Beverly Hills, CA: Sage.

Brislin, R. W., Landis, D., & Brandt, M. E. (1983). Conceptualizations of intercultural behavior and training. In D. Landis & R. W. Brislin (Eds.), *Handbook of intercultural training* (Vol. 1, pp. 1–34). New York: Pergamon.

Brislin, R. W., & Pedersen, P. (1976). *Cross-cultural orientation programs.* New York: Gardner Press.

Brislin, R. W., & Yoshida, T. (Eds.). (1994). *Improving intercultural interaction.* Thousand Oaks, CA: Sage.

Brown, R. J., & Abrams, D. (1986). The effects of intergroup similarity and goal interdependence on intergroup attitudes and task performance. *Journal of Experimental Social Psychology, 22,* 78–92.

Brown v. Board of Education, 347 U.S. 483 (1954).

Bruffee, K. A. (1993). *Collaborative learning.* Baltimore: Johns Hopkins University Press.

Burnstein, E., & McCrae, R. (1962). Some effects of shared threat and prejudice in racially mixed groups. *Journal of Abnormal and Social Psychology, 64,* 257–260.

Burton, J. W. (1974). Conflict resolution. *International Studies Quarterly, 16,* 41–52.

Burton, J. W. (1986). The procedures of conflict resolution. In E. E. Azar & R. W. Burton (Eds.), *International conflict resolution: Theory and practice* (pp. 92–116). Boulder, CO: Lynne Reiner.

Burton, J. W. (1987). *Resolving deep-rooted conflict.* Lantham, MD: University Press of America.

Byrne, D. (1971). *The attraction paradigm.* New York: Academic Press.

Byrnes, D. A., & Kiger, G. (1990). The effect of a prejudice-reduction simulation on attitude change. *Journal of Applied Social Psychology, 20,* 341–356.

Carter, D. E., DeTine, S. L., Spero, J., & Benson, F. W. (1975). Peer acceptance and school related variables in an integrated junior high school. *Journal of Educational Psychology, 67,* 267–273.

Clark, M. S., & Isen, A. M. (1982). Toward understanding the relationship between feeling states and social behavior. In A. H. Hastorf & A. M. Isen (Eds.), *Cognitive social psychology* (pp. 73–108). New York: Elsevier North-Holland.

Cohen, E. (1980). Design and redesign of the desegregated school: Problems of status, power, and conflict. In W. G. Stephan & J. Feagin (Eds.), *School desegregation: Past, present, and future* (pp. 251–280). New York: Plenum.

Cohen, E. (1984). The desegregated school: Problems of status, power and interethnic climate. In N. Miller & M. B. Brewer (Eds.), *Groups in contact: The psychology of desegregation* (pp. 77–96). New York: Academic Press.

Cohen, E. (1986). *Designing groupwork: Strategies for heterogeneous classrooms.* New York: Teachers College Press.

Cohen, E. (1990). Teaching in multiculturally heterogeneous classrooms. *McGill Journal of Education, 26,* 7–22.

Cohen, E. G. (1992). *Restructuring the classroom: Conditions for productive small groups.* Madison: Wisconsin Center for Education Research.

Cohen, E., & Roper, S. (1972). Modification of interracial interaction disability: An application of status characteristics theory. *American Sociological Review, 37,* 643–657.

Cohen, E., et al. (1994). Complex instruction: Higher order thinking in heterogeneous classrooms. In S. Sharan (Ed.), *Handbook of cooperative learning methods.* Westport, CT: Greenwood Press.

Coleman, P. T., & Deutsch, M. (1995). The mediation of interethnic conflict in schools. In W. D. Hawley & A. W. Jackson (Eds.), *Toward a common destiny* (pp. 371–396). San Francisco: Jossey-Bass.

Collett, P. (1971). Training Englishmen in the non-verbal behavior of Arabs. *International Journal of Psychology, 6,* 209–215.

Commins, B., & Lockwood, J. (1978). The effects on intergroup relations of mixing Roman Catholics and Protestants: An experimental investigation. *European Journal of Social Psychology, 8,* 383–386.

Cook, S. W. (1962). The systematic study of socially significant events: A strategy for social research. *Journal of Social Issues, 18,* 66–84.

Cook, S. W. (1979). Social science and school desegregation: Did we mislead the Supreme Court? *Personality and Social Psychology Bulletin, 5,* 420–437.

Cook, S. W. (1984). The 1954 social science statement and school desegregation: A reply to Gerard. *American Psychologist, 39,* 819–832.

Coser, L. (1956). *The functions of social conflict.* New York: Free Press.

Costrich, N.J., Feinstein, L., Kidder, L., Marachek, J., & Pascale, L. (1975). When stereotypes hurt: Three studies of penalties for sex-role reversal. *Journal of Experimental Social Psychology, 11,* 520–530.

Crain, R. (1970). School integration and occupational achievement of Negroes. *American Journal of Sociology, 75,* 593–606.

Crain, R. L., Hawes, J. A., Miller, R. L., & Peichert, J. A. (1985). *Finding niches: Desegregated students 16 years later* (Report R3243–NIE). Santa Monica, CA: Rand Corporation.

Crain, R., & Mahard, R. (1978). School racial composition and black college attendance and achievement test performance. *Sociology of Education, 51,* 81–101.

Crain, R., Mahard, R., & Narot, R. (1982). *Making desegregation work.* Cambridge, MA: Ballinger.

Crain, R., & Straus, J. (1986). *School desegregation and black occupational attainments: Results from a long-term experiment.* Unpublished report, Johns Hopkins University, Baltimore.

Crain, R., & Weisman, C. (1972). *Discrimination, personality and achievement.* New York: Seminar Press.

Crocker, J., Fiske, S. T., & Taylor, S. E. (1984). Schematic bases of belief change. In R. Eiser (Ed.), *Attitude judgment* (pp. 197–226). New York: Springer.

Crocker, J., Hannah, D. B., & Weber, R. (1983). Person memory and causal attributions. *Journal of Personality and Social Psychology, 44,* 55–66.

Crocker, J., & Major, B. (1989). Social stigma and self-esteem: The self-protective properties of stigma. *Psychological Review, 96,* 608–630.

Cross, W. E., Jr. (1995). Oppositional identity and African-American youth: Issues and prospects. In W. D. Hawley & A. W. Jackson (Eds.), *Toward a common destiny* (pp. 185–204). San Francisco: Jossey-Bass.

Cupach, W. R., & Canary, D. J. (1997). *Competence in interpersonal conflict.* New York: McGraw-Hill.

Cushner, K. (1989). Assessing the impact of a culture-general assimilator in intercultural training. *International Journal of Intercultural Relations, 13,* 125–146.

Cushner, K., & Brislin, R. (1996). *Intercultural interaction: A practical guide* (2nd ed.). Thousand Oaks, CA: Sage.

Cushner, K., & Landis, D. (1996). The intercultural sensitizer. In D. Landis & R. S. Bhagat (Eds.), *Handbook of intercultural training* (2nd ed.; pp. 185–202). Thousand Oaks, CA: Sage.

Dardenne, B., & Leyens, J. (1995). Confirmation bias as a social skill. *Personality and Social Psychology Bulletin, 21,* 1229–1239.

Darley, J. M., Fleming, J. H., Hilton, J. L., & Swann, W. B. Jr. (1986). *Dispelling negative expectancies: The impact of interaction goals and target characteristics on the expectation confirmation process.* Unpublished manuscript, Princeton University, Princeton, NJ.

Darley, J. M., & Gross, P. H. (1983). A hypothesis-testing bias in labeling effects. *Journal of Personality and Social Psychology, 44,* 20–43.

Davidson, F. H., & Davidson, M. M. (1994). *Changing childhood prejudice: The caring work of the schools.* Westport, CT: Greenwood Press.

Deaux, K., & Lewis, L. L. (1984). Structure of gender stereotypes: Interrelationships among components and gender label. *Journal of Personality and Social Psychology, 46,* 991–1004.

deDreu, C. K. W., Yzerbyt, V. Y., & Leyens, J. P. (1995). Dilution of stereotype-based cooperation in mixed-motive interdependence. *Journal of Experimental Social Psychology, 31,* 575–593.

Desforges, D. M., Lord, C. G., Ramsey, S. L., Mason, J. A., VanLeeuven, M. D., West, S. C., & Lepper, M. R. (1991). Effects of structured cooperative contact on changing negative attitudes toward stigmatized social groups. *Journal of Personality and Social Psychology, 60,* 531–544.

Deutsch, M. (1949). A theory of cooperation and competition. *Human Relations, 2,* 129–152.

Deutsch, M. (1993). Cooperative learning and conflict resolution in an alternative high school. *Cooperative Learning, 13,* 2–5.

Deutsch, M. (1994). Constructive conflict resolution: Principles, training and research. *Journal of Social Issues, 50,* 13–32.

Devine, P. G. (1989). Stereotypes and prejudice: Their automatic and controlled components. *Journal of Personality and Social Psychology, 56,* 5–18.

Devine, P. G., Hirt, E. R., & Gehrke, E. M. (1990). Diagnostic and confirmation strategies in trait hypothesis testing. *Journal of Personality and Social Psychology, 58,* 952–963.

Devine, P. G., Monteith, M. J., Zuwerink, J. R., & Elliot, A. J. (1991). Prejudice with and without compunction. *Journal of Personality and Social Psychology, 60,* 817–830.

DeVries, D. L., & Edwards, K. J. (1974). Student teams and learning games: Their effects on cross-race and cross-sex interaction. *Journal of Educational Psychology, 66,* 741–749.

DeVries, D. L., Edwards, K. J., & Slavin, R. E. (1978). Biracial learning teams and race relations in the classroom: Four field experiments on Teams–Games–Tournaments. *Journal of Educational Psychology, 70,* 356–362.

Dinnerstein, L., Nichols, R. L., & Reimers, D. M. (1996). *Natives and strangers: A multicultural history of Americans* (3rd ed.). New York: Oxford University Press.

Doob, L. W. (1974). A Cyprus workshop: An exercise in intervention methodology. *Journal of Social Psychology, 84,* 161–178.

Dovidio, J. F., Evans, N., & Tyler, R. B. (1986). Racial stereotypes: The contents and their cognitive representation. *Journal of Experimental Social Psychology, 22,* 22–37.

Dovidio, J. F., & Gaertner, S. L. (1981). The effects of race, status, and ability on helping behavior. *Social Psychology Quarterly, 44,* 192–203.

Dovidio, J. F., & Gaertner, S. L. (1983). Race, normative structure, and help-seeking. In B. M. DePaulo, A. Nadler, & J. D. Fisher (Eds.), *New directions in helping* (Vol. 2, pp. 286–302). New York: Academic Press.

Dovidio, J. F., Gaertner, S. L., Isen, A. M., & Lowrance, R. (1995). Group presentations and intergroup bias: Positive affect, similarity, and group size. *Personality and Social Psychology Bulletin, 21,* 856–865.

Duckitt, J. (1992a). Psychology and prejudice: A historical analysis and integrative framework. *American Psychologist, 47,* 1182–1193.

Duckitt, J. (1992b). *The social psychology of prejudice.* New York: Praeger.

Duncan, B. (1976). Differential social perception and attribution of intergroup violence: Testing the lower limits of stereotyping blacks. *Journal of Personality and Social Psychology, 34,* 590–598.

Dutta, S., Kanungo, R. N., & Freibergs, V. (1972). Retention of affective material: Effects of intensity of affect on retrieval. *Journal of Personality and Social Psychology, 23,* 65–80.

Eagly, A. H., & Chaiken, S. (1992). *The psychology of attitudes.* San Diego, CA: Harcourt Brace Jovanovich.

Eagly, A. H., & Mladinic, A. (1989). Gender stereotypes and attitudes toward men and women. *Personality and Social Psychology Bulletin, 15,* 543–558.

Ellison, C. G., & Powers, D. A. (1994). The contact hypothesis and racial attitudes among black Americans. *Social Science Quarterly, 75,* 385–400.

Epstein, J. A., & Harackiewicz, J. M. (1992). Winning is not enough: The effects of competition and achievement orientation on intrinsic interest. *Personality and Social Psychology Bulletin, 18,* 128–138.

Epstein, J. L. (1985). After the bus arrives: Resegregation in desegregated schools. *Journal of Social Issues, 41,* 23–43.

Erber, R. (1991). Affective and semantic priming: Effects of mood on category accessibility and inference. *Journal of Experimental Social Psychology, 27,* 480–498.

Erber, R., & Fiske, S. T. (1984). Outcome dependency and attention to inconsistent information. *Journal of Personality and Social Psychology, 47,* 709–726.

Eshel, S., & Peres, Y. (1973). The integration of a minority group: A causal model. Cited in Y. Amir (1976), The role of intergroup contact in change of prejudice and race relations. In P. A. Katz (Ed.), *Towards the elimination of racism* (pp. 245–308). New York: Pergamon.

Esses, V. M., Haddock, G., & Zanna, M. P. (1993a). Attitudes, stereotypes, and emotions as determinants of intergroup attitudes. In D. M. Mackie & D. L. Hamilton (Eds.), *Affect, cognition, and stereotyping: Interactive processes in group perception* (pp.137–166). San Diego: Academic Press.

Esses, V. M., Haddock, G., & Zanna, M. P. (1993b). The role of mood in the expression of intergroup stereotypes. In M. P. Zanna & J. M. Olsen (Eds.), *The psychology of prejudice: The Ontario symposium* (pp. 77–101). Hillsdale, NJ: Erlbaum.

Farley, R. (1985). Three steps forward and two back? Recent changes in the social and economic status of blacks. In R. D. Alba (Ed.), *Ethnicity and race in the U.S.A.* (pp. 4–28). Boston: Routledge & Kegan Paul.

Fazio, R. H., Effrein, E. A., & Falender, V. J. (1981). Self-perceptions following social interaction. *Journal of Personality and Social Psychology, 41,* 232–242.

Fein, S., & Spencer, S. J. (1997). Prejudice as self-image maintenance: Affirming the self through derogating others. *Journal of Personality and Social Psychology, 73,* 31–44.

Fine, M. (1993). Collaborative innovations: Documentation of the Facing History and Ourselves program at an essential school. *Teachers College Record, 94,* 771–789.

Fine, M. (1995). *Habits of mind: Struggling over values in America's classrooms.* San Francisco: Jossey-Bass.

Finlay, C. A., & Stephan, W. G. (1997). *Reducing prejudice: The effects of empathy on affect, cognition, and attitude.* Unpublished manuscript, New Mexico State University Las Cruces.

Fisher, R. (1990). *The social psychology of intergroup and international conflict resolution.* New York: Springer-Verlag.

Fisher, R. (1994). General principles for resolving intergroup conflict. *Journal of Social Issues, 50,* 47–66.

Fiske, S. T., & Neuberg, S. L. (1989). Category-based versus piecemeal-based affective responses: Developments in schema-triggered affect. In R. M. Sorrentino and E. T. Higgins (Eds.), *The handbook of motivation and cognition: Foundations of social behavior* (pp. 167–203). New York: Guilford Press.

Fiske, S. T., & Pavelchak, M. A. (1986). Category-based versus piecemeal-based affective responses: Developments in schema-triggered affect. In R. M. Sorrentino & E. T. Higgins (Eds.), *The handbook of motivation and cognition: Foundations of social behavior* (pp. 167–203). New York: Guilford Press.

Fordham, S., & Ogbu, J. (1986). Black students' school success: Coping with the burden of acting white. *The Urban Review, 18,* 176–206.

Frey, D., & Gaertner, S. L. (1986). Helping and the avoidance of inappropriate interracial behavior: A strategy that can perpetuate a non-prejudiced self-image. *Journal of Personality and Social Psychology, 50,* 1083–1090.

Gaertner, S. L., & Dovidio, J. F. (1977). The subtlety of white racism, arousal, and helping behavior. *Journal of Personality and Social Psychology, 35,* 691–707.

Gaertner, S. L., & Dovidio, J. F. (1986). The aversive form of racism. In J. F. Dovidio & S. L. Gaertner (Eds.), *Prejudice, discrimination, and racism* (pp. 61–90). New York: Academic Press.

Gaertner, S. L., Mann, J., Dovidio, J. F., Murrell, A., & Pomare, M. (1990). How does cooperation reduce intergroup bias? *Journal of Personality and Social Psychology, 59,* 692–704.

Gaertner, S. L., Mann, J., Murrell, A., & Dovidio, J. F. (1989). Reducing intergroup bias: The benefits of recategorization. *Journal of Personality and Social Psychology, 57,* 239–249.

Genser, L. (1985). Children's rights and responsibilities: A teaching unit for elementary grades. *Social Education, 49,* 500–503.

Gerard, H. B. (1983). School desegregation: The social science role. *American Psychologist, 38,* 869–877.

Gilbert, D. T. (1989). Thinking lightly about others: Automatic components of the social inference process. In J. S. Uleman & J. A. Bargh (Eds.), *Unintended thought* (pp. 189–211). New York: Guilford Press.

Gilbert, D. T., & Hixon, G. (1991). The trouble of thinking: Activation and application of stereotypic beliefs. *Journal of Personality and Social Psychology, 60,* 509–517.

Gonzales, A. (1979, August). *Classroom cooperation and ethnic balance.* Paper presented at the annual convention of the American Psychological Association, New York.

Gonzales, N. A., & Cauce, A. M. (1995). Ethnic identity and multicultural competence: Dilemmas and challenges for youth. In W. D. Hawley & A. W. Jackson (Eds.), *Toward a common destiny* (pp. 131–162). San Francisco: Jossey-Bass.

Goodman, M. E. (1952). *Race awareness in young children.* Cambridge, MA: Addison-Wesley.

Grant, C. A., & Grant, G. W. (1985). Staff development and education that is multicultural. *British Journal of In-Service Education, 12,* 6–18.

Grant, C. A., & Sleeter, C. E. (1989). *Turning on learning.* New York: Macmillan.

Grant, C. A., & Tate, W. F. (1995). Multicultural education through the lens of the multicultural education research literature. In J. A. Banks & C. A. McGee Banks (Eds.), *Handbook of research on multicultural education* (pp. 145–165). New York: Macmillan.

Grant, P. R., & Holmes, J. G. (1981). The integration of implicit personality theory, schemas, and stereotype images. *Social Psychology Quarterly, 44,* 107–115.

Gray, D. B., & Ashmore, R. D. (1975). Comparing the effects of informational, role-playing, and value-discrepant treatments of racial attitudes. *Journal of Applied Social Psychology, 5,* 262–281.

Green, K. (1981, February). *Integration and achievement: Preliminary results from a longitudinal study of educational attainment among black students.* Paper presented at the meeting of the American Educational Research Association, Chicago.

Greenberg, J., Pysczynski, T., Solomon, S., & Rosenblatt, A., Veeder, M., Kirkland, S., & Lyon, D. (1990). Evidence for terror management theory II: The effects of mortality salience on reactions to those who threaten or bolster the cultural worldview. *Journal of Personality and Social Psychology, 58,* 308–318.

Greenberg, J., Simon, L., Pysczynski, T., Solomon, S., & Chatel, D. (1992). Terror management and tolerance: Does mortality salience always intensify negative reactions to others who threaten one's worldview. *Journal of Personality and Social Psychology, 63,* 212–220.

Gudykunst, W. B. (1988). Uncertainty and anxiety. In Y. Y. Kim & W. B. Gudykunst (Eds.), *Theories in intercultural communication.* Newbury Park, CA: Sage.

Gudykunst, W. B., & Hammer, M. R. (1983). Basic training design: Approaches to intercultural training. In D. Landis & R. W. Brislin (Eds.), *Handbook of intercultural training* (Vol. 1, pp. 118–154). New York: Pergamon.

Hallinan, M. T., & Smith, S. S. (1985). The effects of classroom composition on students' interracial friendliness. *Social Psychology Quarterly, 48,* 3–16.

Hallinan, M. T., & Teixeira, R. A. (1987). Students' interracial friendships: Individual characteristics, structural effects, and racial differences. *American Journal of Education, 95,* 563–583.

Hamilton, D. L., & Rose, T. (1980). Illusory correlation and the maintenance of stereotype beliefs. *Journal of Personality and Social Psychology, 39,* 832–845.

Hamilton, D. L., Sherman, S. J., & Ruvolo, C. M. (1990). Stereotype-based expectancies: Effects on information processing and social behavior. *Journal of Personality and Social Psychology, 46,* 35–60.

Harding, J., Kutner, B., Proshansky, N., & Chein, I. (1954). Prejudice and ethnic relations. In G. Lindzey (Ed.), *Handbook of social psychology* (Vol. II, pp. 1021–1061). Cambridge, MA: Addison–Wesley.

Harris and Associates. (1989). *The unfinished agenda on race in America* (Report submitted to the NAACP Legal Defense and Education Fund). Cited in G. Orfield & S. E. Eaton (1996), *Dismantling desegregation.* New York: New Press.

Harris, M. J., Milich, R., Corbitt, E. M., Hoover, D. W., & Brady, M. (1992). Self-fulfilling effects of stigmatizing information on children's social interactions. *Journal of Personality and Social Psychology, 63,* 41–50.

Haslam, A. S., Oakes, P. J., Turner, J. C., & McGarty, C. (1996). Social identity, self-categorization, and the perceived homogeneity of ingroups and out-groups: The interaction between social motivation and cognition. In R. M. Sorrentino & E. T. Higgins (Eds.), *Handbook of motivation and cognition* (Vol. 3, pp. 182–224). New York: Guilford Press.

Hastie, R., & Kumar, A. P. (1979). Person memory: Personality traits as organizing principles in memory for behaviors. *Journal of Personality and Social Psychology, 37,* 25–38.

Hauserman, N., Walen, S. R., & Behling, M. (1973). Reinforced racial integration in the first grade: A study of generalization. *Journal of Applied Behavioral Analysis, 6,* 193–200.

Hemsley, G. D., & Marmurek, H. V. C. (1982). Person memory: The processing of consistent and inconsistent person information. *Personality and Social Psychology Bulletin, 8,* 433–438.

Henderson-King, E. I., & Nisbett, R. E. (1996). Anti-black prejudice as a function of exposure to the negative behavior of a single black person. *Journal of Personality and Social Psychology, 71,* 654–664.

Hertz-Lazarowitz, R., & Miller, N. (Eds.). (1992). *Interaction in cooperative groups.* New York: Cambridge University Press.

Hertz-Lazarowitz, R., Sapir, C., & Sharan, S. (1982). The effects of two cooperative learning methods and traditional teaching on the achievement and social relations of pupils in mixed ethnic junior high school classes. Cited in J. Schwarzwald & Y. Amir (1984), Interethnic relations and education: An Israeli perspective. In N. Miller & M. B. Brewer (Eds.), *Groups in contact: The psychology of desegregation* (pp. 53–76). New York: Academic Press.

Hewstone, M. (1990). The "ultimate attribution error"? A review of literature on intergroup causal attribution. *European Journal of Social Psychology, 20,* 311–335.

Hewstone, M., & Brown, R. (1986). Contact is not enough: An intergroup perspective on the contact hypothesis. In M. Hewstone & R. Brown (Eds.),

Contact and conflict in intergroup encounters (pp. 1–44). Oxford: Basil Blackwell.

Hewstone, M., Hopkins, N., & Routh, D. A. (1992). Cognitive models of stereotype change: I. Generalization and subtyping in young people's views of the police. *European Journal of Social Psychology, 22,* 219–234.

Hewstone, M., Islam, M. R., & Judd, C. M. (1993). Models of crossed categorization and intergroup relations. *Journal of Personality and Social Psychology, 64,* 779–793.

Hewstone, M., & Jaspars, H. (1982). Intergroup relations and attribution processes. In H. Tajfel (Ed.), *Social identity and intergroup relations.* Cambridge: Cambridge University Press.

Higgins, E. T., & King, G. (1981). Accessibility of social constructs: Information processing consequences of individual and contextual variables. In N. Cantor & J. F. Kihlstrom (Eds.), *Personality, cognition, and social interaction* (pp. 69–122). Hillsdale, NJ: Erlbaum.

Higgins, E. T., & Rholes, W. S. (1978). "Saying is believing": Effects of message modification on memory and liking for the person described. *Journal of Experimental Social Psychology, 14,* 363–378.

Hilton, J. L., & Fein, S. (1989). The role of typical diagnosticity in stereotype-based judgments. *Journal of Personality and Social Psychology, 57,* 501–511.

Hilton, J. L., & von Hippel, W. (1990). The role of consistency in the judgment of stereotype-relevant behaviors. *Personality and Social Psychology Bulletin, 16,* 430–448.

Hoffman, E. (1985). The effects of race-ratio composition on the frequency of organizational communication. *Social Psychology Quarterly, 48,* 17–26.

Hohn, R. L. (1973). Perceptual training and its effects on racial preferences in kindergarten children. *Psychological Reports, 32,* 435–441.

Ijaz, M. A. (1984). Ethnic attitude change. In R. J. Samuda, J. W. Berry, & M. Laferriere (Eds.), *Multiculturalism in Canada* (pp. 128–138). Toronto: Allyn & Bacon.

Isen, A. M. (1982). Some perspectives on cognitive social psychology. In A. H. Hastorf & A. M. Isen (Eds.), *Cognitive social psychology* (pp. 1–31). New York: Elsevier North-Holland.

Isen, A. M. (1984). Toward understanding the role of affect in cognition. In R. S. Wyer & T. K. Srull (Eds.), *Handbook of social cognition* (Vol. 2, pp. 179–236). Hillsdale, NJ: Erlbaum.

Islam, M. R., & Hewstone, M. (1993). Dimensions of contact as predictors of intergroup anxiety, perceived outgroup variability, and out-group attitude: An integrative model. *Personality and Social Psychology Bulletin, 19,* 700–710.

Jackman, M. R., & Crane, M. (1986). "Some of my best friends are black . . .": Interracial friendship and whites' racial attitudes. *Public Opinion Quarterly, 50,* 459–486.

Jackson, L. A., & Cash, T. F. (1985). Components of gender stereotypes and their implications for stereotype and nonstereotype judgments. *Personality and Social Psychology Bulletin, 11,* 326–344.

James, W. (1890). *The principles of psychology.* New York: Holt.

Johnson, D. W., & Johnson, R. T. (1992a). Positive interdependence: Key to effective cooperation. In R. Hertz-Lazarowitz & N. Miller (Eds.), *Interaction in cooperative groups* (pp. 174–199). New York: Cambridge University Press.

Johnson, D. W., & Johnson, R. T. (1992b). Social interdependence and cross-ethnic relationships. In J. Lynch, C. Modgil, & S. Modgil (Eds.), *Cultural diversity in the schools* (Vol. II, pp. 179–190). London: Falmer Press.

Johnson, D. W., & Johnson, R. T. (1995a). *My mediation notebook* (3rd ed.). Edina, MN: Interaction Book Co.

Johnson, D. W., & Johnson, R. T. (1995b). *Teaching students to be peacemakers* (3rd ed.). Edina, MN: Interaction Book Co.

Johnson, D. W., Johnson, R. T., Dudley, B., & Acikgoz, K. (1994). Effects of conflict resolution training on elementary school students. *Journal of Social Psychology, 134,* 803–817.

Johnson, D. W., Johnson, R. T., Dudley, B., & Magnusson, D. (1995). Training elementary school students to manage conflict. *Journal of Social Psychology, 135,* 673–686.

Johnson, D. W., Johnson, R. T., & Holubec, E. J. (1994). *Cooperative learning in the classroom.* Alexandria, VA: Association for Supervision and Curriculum Development.

Johnson, D. W., Johnson, R., & Maruyama, G. (1984). Goal interdependence and interpersonal attraction in heterogeneous classrooms. In N. Miller & M. B. Brewer (Eds.), *Groups in contact: The psychology of desegregation* (pp. 187–213). New York: Academic Press.

Johnson, R. C., & Nagoshi, C. (1986). The adjustment of offspring of within-group and interracial/intercultural marriages: A comparison of personality factor scores. *Journal of Marriage and the Family, 48,* 279–284.

Johnston, L. (1996). Resisting change: Information seeking and stereotype change. *European Journal of Social Psychology, 26,* 799–825.

Johnston, L., & Hewstone, M. (1992). Cognitive models of stereotype change. *Journal of Experimental Social Psychology, 28,* 360–386.

Jones, E. E., & Nisbett, R. E. (1971). The actor and the observer: Divergent perceptions of the causes of behavior. In E. E. Jones, D. Kanouse, H. H. Kelley, R. E. Nisbett, S. Valins, & B. Weiner (Eds.), *Attribution: Perceiving the causes of behavior* (pp. 79–94). Morristown, NJ: General Learning Press.

Jones, J. M. (1991). Bicultural strategies for coping with prejudice and racism. In H. J. Knopke, R. J. Norrell, & R. W. Rogers (Eds.), *Opening doors: Perspectives on race relations in contemporary America* (pp. 179–197). Tuscaloosa: University of Alabama Press.

Jones, J. M. (1997). *Prejudice and racism* (2nd ed.). New York: McGraw-Hill.

Jost, J. T., & Banaji, M. R. (1993). The role of stereotyping in system-justification and the production of false consciousness. *British Journal of Social Psychology, 33,* 1–27.

Kagan, J. (1980). Cooperation–competition, culture, and structural bias in classrooms. In S. Sharon, P. Hare, C. D. Webb, & R. Hertz-Lazarowitz (Eds.), *Coop-*

eration in education (pp. 197–211). Provo, UT: Brigham Young University Press.

Kamfer, L., & Venter, J. L. (1994). First evaluation of a stereotype reduction workshop. *South African Journal of Psychology, 24,* 13–20.

Katz, I., Glass, D.C., & Cohen, S. (1973). Ambivalence, guilt, and the scapegoating of minority group victims. *Journal of Experimental Social Psychology, 9,* 423–436.

Katz, I., Glass, D.C., Lucido, D. J., & Farber, J. (1979). Harm-doing and victim's racial or orthopedic stigma as determinants of helping behavior. *Journal of Personality, 47,* 430–464.

Katz, I., Glass, D.C., & Wackenhut, J. (1986). An ambivalence-amplification theory of behavior toward the stigmatized. In S. Worchel & W. G. Austin (Eds.), *Psychology of intergroup relations* (2nd ed.; pp. 103–117). Chicago: Nelson-Hall.

Katz, I., Wackenhut, J., & Hass, R. G. (1986). Racial ambivalence, value duality, and behavior. In J. F. Dovidio & S. L. Gaertner (Eds.), *Prejudice, discrimination, and racism* (pp. 35–60). New York: Academic Press.

Katz, J. H., & Ivey, A. (1977). White awareness: The frontier of race awareness training. *Personnel Guidance, 55,* 485–489.

Katz, P. A. (1976). The acquisition of racial attitudes. In P. A. Katz (Ed.), *Towards the elimination of racism* (pp. 3–20). New York: Pergamon.

Kehoe, J. W., & Rogers, T. W. (1978). The effects of principle testing discussions on student attitudes toward selected groups subject to discrimination. *Canadian Journal of Education, 3,* 73–80.

Kelley, H. H. (1967). Attribution theory in social psychology. In D. Levine (Ed.), *Nebraska symposium on motivation* (Vol. 15, pp. 192–238). Lincoln: University of Nebraska Press.

Kelman, H. C. (1990). Interactive problem-solving: A social psychological approach to conflict resolution. In J. Burton & F. Dukes (Eds.), *Conflict: Readings in management and resolution* (pp. 199–215). New York: St. Martin's Press.

Kelman, H. C., & Cohen, S. P. (1986). Resolution of international conflict: An interactional approach. In S. Worchel & W. G. Austin (Eds.), *Psychology of intergroup relations* (2nd ed., pp. 323–332). Chicago: Nelson-Hall.

Kelman, H., & Pettigrew, T. (1959). How to understand prejudice. *Commentary, 28,* 436–441.

Kendall, F. E. (1983). *Diversity in the classroom: A multicultural approach to the education of young children.* New York: Teachers College Press.

Kohlberg, L. (1969). Stage and sequence: The cognitive developmental approach to socialization. In D. A. Goslin (Ed.), *Handbook of socialization theory and research* (pp. 379–421). Chicago: Rand McNally.

Kohlberg, L. (1981). *Essays on moral development.* New York: Harper & Row.

Krueger, J., & Rothbart, M. (1988). Use of categorical and individuating information in making inferences about personality. *Journal of Personality and Social Psychology, 55,* 187–195.

Kulik, J. (1983). Confirmatory attribution and the perpetuation of social beliefs. *Journal of Personality and Social Psychology, 44,* 1171–1181.

Kunda, Z., & Oleson, K. C. (1995). Maintaining stereotypes in the face of discon-firmation: Constructing grounds for subtyping deviants. *Journal of Personality and Social Psychology, 68,* 565–579.

Landis, D., Brislin, R. W., & Hulgus, J. F. (1985). Attributional training versus con-tact in acculturative learning: A laboratory study. *Journal of Applied Social Psychology, 15,* 466–482.

Landis, D., Day, H. R., McGrew, P. L., Thomas, J. A., & Miller, A. B. (1976). Can a "black" cultural assimilator increase racial understanding? *Journal of Social Issues, 32,* 169–183.

Langer, E. J., Bashner, R. S., & Chanowitz, B. (1985). Decreasing prejudice by increasing discrimination. *Journal of Personality and Social Psychology, 49,* 113–120.

LeVine, R. A., & Campbell, D. T. (1972). *Ethnocentrism: Theories of conflict, ethnic attitudes, and group behavior.* New York: Wiley.

Lewin, K. (1944). Constructs in psychology and psychological ecology. *University of Iowa Studies in Child Welfare, 20,* 23–27.

Linville, P. W. (1982). The complexity-extremity effect and age-based stereotyp-ing. *Journal of Personality and Social Psychology, 42,* 192–211.

Linville, P. W., Salovey, P., & Fischer, G. W. (1986). Stereotyping and perceived distributions of social characteristics: An application to ingroup–outgroup perception. In J. F. Dovidio & S. L. Gaertner (Eds.), *Prejudice, discrimination, and racism* (pp. 165–208). New York: Academic Press.

Locksley, A., Borgida, E., Brekke, N., & Hepburn, C. A. (1980). Sex stereotypes and social judgment. *Journal of Personality and Social Psychology, 39,* 821–831.

Locksley, A., Hepburn, C., & Ortiz, V. (1982). Social stereotypes and the judg-ment of individuals: An instance of the base-rate fallacy. *Journal of Experi-mental Social Psychology, 18,* 23–42.

Longshore, D. (1982). School racial composition and blacks' attitudes toward desegregation: The problem of control in desegregated schools. *Social Sci-ence Quarterly, 63,* 674–687.

Looking for America: Vol. 1. Promising school based practices in intergroup rela-tions, (1994). Boston: National Coalition of Advocates for Students.

Lopez, G. E., Gurin, P., & Nagda, B. A. (1998). *Education and understanding struc-tural causes for group inequalities.* Unpublished manuscript, University of Michigan, Ann Arbor.

Lord, C. G., Lepper, M. R., & Preston, E. (1984). Considering the opposite: A cor-rective strategy for social judgment. *Journal of Personality and Social Psy-chology, 47,* 1231–1243.

Lucker, G. W., Rosenfield, D., Aronson, E., & Sikes, J. (1977). Performance in the interdependent classroom. *American Educational Research Journal, 13,* 115–123.

Mackie, D. M., Allison, S. T., Worth, L. T., & Asuncion, A. G. (1992). Social decision making processes: The generalization of outcome-biased counter-stereotypic inferences. *Journal of Experimental Social Psychology, 28,* 23–42.

Mackie, D. M., Hamilton, D. L., Schroth, H. A., Carlisle, C. J., Gersho, B. F., Meneses, L. M., Nedler, B. F., & Reichel, L. D. (1989). The effects of induced mood on expectancy-based illusory correlations. *Journal of Experimental Social Psychology, 25,* 524–544.

Mackie, D. M., Queller, S., Stroessner, S. J., & Hamilton, D. L. (1996). Making stereotypes better or worse: Multiple roles of positive affect in group impressions. In R. M. Sorrentino & E. T. Higgins (Eds.), *Handbook of social cognition* (Vol. 3, pp. 371–396). New York: Guilford Press.

Mahan, J. M. (1982). Community involvement components in culturally-oriented teacher preparation. *Education, 103,* 163–172.

Mahan, J. M. (1984). Major concerns of Anglo student teachers serving in native-American communities. *Journal of American Indian Education, 23,* 19–24.

Major, B., Cozarelli, C., Testa, M., & McFarlin, D. B. (1988). Self-verification versus expectancy-confirmation in social interaction: The impact of self-focus. *Personality and Social Psychology Bulletin, 14,* 346–359.

Maslow, A. H. (1970). *Motivation and personality.* New York: Harper & Row.

Masson, C. N., & Verkuyten, M. (1993). Prejudice, ethnicity, contact and ethnic group preferences among Dutch young adolescents. *Journal of Applied Social Psychology, 23,* 156–168.

Mayer, J. D. (1989). How mood influences cognition. In N. E. Sharkey (Ed.), *Advances in cognitive science* (Vol. I, pp. 290–313). New York: Wiley.

Mayer, J. D., Gayle, M., Meehan, M. E., & Haarman, A. (1990). Toward better specification of the mood-consistency effect in recall. *Journal of Experimental Social Psychology, 26,* 465–480.

Mayer, J. D., & Salovey, P. (1988). Personality moderates the interaction of mood and cognition. In K. Fiedler & J. Forgas (Eds.), *Affect, cognition and social behavior* (pp. 87–99). Toronto: Hogrefe.

McArthur, L. Z. (1982). Judging a book by its cover: A cognitive analysis of the relationship between physical appearance and stereotyping. In A. H. Hastorf & A. M. Isen (Eds.), *Cognitive social psychology.* New York: Elsevier North-Holland.

McArthur, L. Z., & Post, D. L. (1977). Figural emphasis and person perception. *Journal of Personality and Social Psychology, 39,* 625–634.

McArthur, L. Z., & Soloman, L. K. (1978). Perceptions of an aggressive encounter as a function of the victim's salience and the perceiver's arousal. *Journal of Experimental Social Psychology, 13,* 520–535.

McClendon, M. J. (1974). Interracial contact and the reduction of prejudice. *Sociological Focus, 7,* 47–65.

McConahay, J. G. (1986). Modern racism, ambivalence, and the modern racism scale. In J. F. Dovidio & S. L. Gaertner (Eds.), *Prejudice, discrimination, and racism* (pp. 91–125). New York: Academic Press.

McConahay, J., & Hawley, W. (1976). *Attitudes of Louisville and Jefferson County citizens toward busing for public school desegregation.* Unpublished report, Duke University, Durham, NC.

McGee Banks, C. A. (1995). Parents and teachers, partners in school reform. In J. A. Banks & C. A. McGee Banks (Eds.), *Multicultural education: Issues and perspectives* (2nd ed.; pp. 332–352). Boston: Allyn & Bacon. (Original work published 1993)

McGregor, J. (1993). Effectiveness of role-playing and antiracist teaching in reducing student prejudice. *Journal of Educational Research, 86,* 215–226.

Merton, R. K. (1948). The self-fulfilling prophecy. *Antioch Review, 8,* 193–210.

Miller, N., Brewer, M. B., & Edwards, K. (1985). Cooperative interaction in desegregated settings: A laboratory analogue. *Journal of Social Issues, 41,* 63–81.

Miller, N., & Davidson-Podgorny, G. (1987). Theoretical models of intergroup relations and the use of cooperative teams as an intervention for desegregated settings. In C. Hendrick (Ed.), *Group processes and intergroup relations* (Vol. 9, pp. 41–67).

Miller, N., & Harrington, H. J. (1990). A model of category salience for intergroup relations: Empirical tests of the relevant variables. In P. J. D. Drenth, J. A. Sargeant, & R. J. Takens (Eds.), *European perspectives in psychology* (Vol. 3, pp. 205–220). New York: Wiley.

Miller, N., & Harrington, H. J. (1992). Social categorization and intergroup acceptance: Principles for the design and development of cooperative learning teams. In R. Hertz-Lazarowitz & N. Miller (Eds.), *Interaction in cooperative groups* (pp. 203–227). New York: Cambridge University Press.

Monteith, M. J. (1993). Self-regulation of prejudiced responses: Implications for progress in prejudice-reduction efforts. *Journal of Personality and Social Psychology, 65,* 469–485.

Monteith, M. J., Devine, P. G., & Zuwerink, J. R. (1993). Self-directed versus other-directed affect as a consequence of prejudice-related discrepancies. *Journal of Personality and Social Psychology, 64,* 198–210.

Monteith, M. J., Zuwerink, J. R., & Devine, P. G. (1994). Prejudice and prejudice reduction: Classic challenges, contemporary approaches. In P. G. Devine, D. L. Hamilton, & T. M. Ostrom (Eds.), *Social cognition: Impact on social psychology* (pp. 324–346). San Diego: Academic Press.

Myrdal, G. (1944). *An American dilemma: The Negro problem and modern democracy.* New York: Random House.

NCSS Task Force. (1992, September). Curriculum guidelines for multicultural education. *Social Education,* pp. 274–294.

Neidenthal, P. M. (1990). Implicit perception of affective information. *Journal of Experimental Social Psychology, 26,* 505–527.

Neuberg, S. L. (1986). Social motives and expectancy-tinged social interactions. In R. M. Sorrentino & E. T. Higgins (Eds.), *The handbook of motivation and cognition* (Vol. 3, pp. 225–261). New York: Guilford Press.

Neuberg, S. L. (1989). The goal of forming accurate impressions during social interaction: Attenuating the impact of negative expectancies. *Journal of Personality and Social Psychology, 56,* 374–386.

Neuberg, S. L. (1996). Social motives and expectancy-tinged thoughts. In R. M. Sorrentino & E. T. Higgins (Eds.), *Handbook of social cognition* (Vol. 3, pp. 225–261). New York: Guilford Press.

Neuberg, S. L., Judice, T. N., Virdin, L. M., & Carillo, M. A. (1993). Perceiver self-presentation goals as moderators of expectancy influences: Ingratiation and disconfirmation of negative expectancies. *Journal of Personality and Social Psychology, 64,* 409–420.

Newcomb, T., Turner, R., & Converse, E. (1965). *Social psychology.* New York: Holt, Rinehart, & Winston.

Nieto, S. (1994). Lessons from students on creating a chance to dream. *Harvard Educational Review, 64,* 392–426.

Nieto, S. (1995). From brown heroes and holidays to assimilationist agendas: Reconsidering the critiques of multicultural education. In C. E. Sleeter & P. L. McLaren (Eds.), *Multicultural education: Critical pedagogy and the politics of difference* (pp. 191–220). Albany: State University of New York Press.

Noordhoff, K., & Kleinfeld, J. (1993). Preparing teachers for multicultural classrooms. *Teaching and Teacher Education, 9,* 27–39.

Norvel, N., & Worchel, S. (1981). A re-examination of the relation between equal-status contact and intergroup attraction. *Journal of Personality and Social Psychology, 41,* 902–908.

Okihiro, G. Y. (1993). The victimization of Asian in America. In *The world and I* (pp. 397–413). Washington, DC: Washington Times.

Olson, J. M., & Zanna, M. P. (1993). Attitudes and attitude change. *Annual Review of Psychology, 44,* 117–154.

Orfield, G. (1980). School desegregation and residential segregation: A social science statement. In W. G. Stephan & J. Feagin (Eds.), *School desegregation: Past, present, and future* (pp. 227–248). New York: Plenum.

Orfield, G., & Eaton, S. F. (1996). *Dismantling desegregation.* New York: New Press.

Osgood, C. E. (1959). Suggestions for winning the real war with communism. *Journal of Conflict Resolution, 3,* 295–325.

Ostrom, T. M., Carpenter, S. L., Sedikides, C., & Li, F. (1993). Differential processing of ingroup and outgroup information. *Journal of Personality and Social Psychology, 64,* 21–34.

Palomares, U., Logan, B., Weber, J., Willson, S., & Kellison, C. (1975). *A curriculum for conflict management.* San Diego: Human Development Training Institute.

Parsons, M. A. (1986). Attitude changes following desegregation in New Castle County, Delaware. In R. L. Green (Ed.), *Metropolitan desegregation* (pp. 185–210). New York: Plenum.

Patchen, M. (1982). *Black–white contact in the schools: Its social and academic effects.* West Lafayette, IN: Purdue University Press.

Patchen, M. (1988). *Resolving disputes between nations: Coercion or conciliation.* Durham, NC: Duke University Press.

Pearce, D. (1980). *Breaking down barriers: New evidence on the impact of metro-*

politan school desegregation on housing patterns. Washington, DC: National Institute of Education.

Pettigrew, T. F. (1969). Racially separate or together? *Journal of Social Issues, 25,* 43–69.

Pettigrew, T. F. (1975). *Racial discrimination in the United States.* New York: Harper & Row.

Pettigrew, T. F. (1979a). Racial change and social policy. *Annals, 441,* 114–131.

Pettigrew, T. F. (1979b). The ultimate attribution error: Extending Allport's cognitive analysis of prejudice. *Personality and Social Psychology Bulletin, 5,* 461–476.

Pettigrew, T. F. (1986). The intergroup contact hypothesis reconsidered. In M. Hewstone & R. Brown (Eds.), *Contact and conflict in intergroup encounters* (pp. 169–195). Oxford: Basil Blackwell.

Phinney, J. S., & Rotheram, M. J. (1987). *Children's ethnic socialization: Pluralism and development.* Newbury Park, CA: Sage.

Ponterotto, J. G., & Pedersen, P. (1993). *Preventing prejudice.* Newbury Park, CA: Sage.

Posner, M. I., & Snyder, C. R. R. (1975). Attention and cognitive control. In R. L. Solso (Ed.), *Information processing and cognition* (pp. 55–86). Hillsdale, NJ: Erlbaum.

Pratto, F., & Bargh, J. A. (1991). Stereotyping based on apparently individuating information: Trait and global components of sex stereotypes under attention overload. *Journal of Experimental Psychology, 27,* 26–47.

Pratto, F., Sidanius, J., Stallworth, L. M., & Malle, B. F. (1994). Social dominance orientation: A personality variable relevant to social roles and intergroup relations. *Journal of Personality and Social Psychology, 67,* 741–763.

Quattrone, G. A. (1986). On the perception of a group's variability. In S. Worchel & W. G. Austin (Eds.), *Psychology of intergroup relations* (2nd ed.; pp. 25–48). Chicago: Nelson-Hall.

Ramsey, P. G. (1987). *Teaching and learning in a diverse world: Multicultural education for young children.* New York: Teachers College Press.

Rasinski, K. A., Crocker, J., & Hastie, R. (1985). Another look at sex stereotypes and social judgments: An analysis of the social perceiver's use of subjective probabilities. *Journal of Personality and Social Psychology, 49,* 327–337.

Riordan, C. (1978). Equal-status interracial contact: A review and revision of the concept. *International Journal of Intercultural Relations, 2,* 161–185.

Rokeach, M. (1971). Long–range experimental modification of values, attitudes and behavior. *American Psychologist, 26,* 453–459.

Root, M. P. P. (1992). *Racially mixed people in America.* Thousand Oaks, CA: Sage.

Rosenfield, D., & Stephan, W. G. (1981). Intergroup relations among children. In S. Brehm, S. Kassin, & F. Gibbons (Eds.), *Developmental social psychology* (pp. 271–297). New York: Oxford University Press.

Rosenfield, D., Stephan, W. G., & Lucker, G. W. (1981). Attraction to competent and incompetent members of cooperative and competitive groups. *Journal of Applied Social Psychology, 11,* 416–433.

Ross, M. H. (1993). *The management of conflict.* New Haven: Yale University Press.

Rossell, C. H. (1978). School desegregation and community social change. *Law and Contemporary Problems, 42,* 133–183.

Rothbart, M., Evans, M., & Fulero, S. (1979). Recall of confirming events: Memory processes and the maintenance of social stereotypes. *Journal of Experimental Social Psychology, 15,* 343–355.

Rothbart, M., & John, O. P. (1985). Social categorization and behavioral episodes: A cognitive analysis and the effects of intergroup contact. *Journal of Social Issues, 41,* 81–104.

Rothbart, M., & Lewis, S. (1988). Inferring category attributes from exemplar attributes: Geometric shapes and social categories. *Journal of Personality and Social Psychology, 55,* 157–178.

Rouhana, N. N., & Kelman, H. C. (1994). Promoting joint thinking in international conflicts: An Israeli–Palestinian continuing workshop. *Journal of Social Issues, 50,* 157–178.

Roy, P. (1994). Cultivating cooperative group process skills within the social studies curriculum. In R. R. Stahl (Ed.), *Cooperative learning in social studies* (pp. 18–50). Menlo Park, CA: Addison-Wesley.

Rumelhart, D. E., Hinton, G. E., & McClelland, J. L. (1986). A general framework for parallel distributed processing. In D. E. Rumelhart, J. L. McClelland, & the PDP Research Group (Eds.), *Parallel distributed processing* (pp. 45–76). Cambridge, MA: MIT Press.

Sagar, H. A., & Schofield, J. W. (1980). Racial and behavioral cues in black and white children's perceptions of ambiguously aggressive acts. *Journal of Personality and Social Psychology, 39,* 590–598.

Sagiv, L., & Schwartz, S. H. (1995). Value priorities and readiness for out-group contact. *Journal of Personality and Social Psychology, 69,* 437–448.

Sanbonmatsu, D. M., Sherman, S. J., & Hamilton, D. L. (1987). Illusory correlation in the perception of individuals and groups. *Social Cognition, 5,* 518–543.

Sarocho, O. N., & Spodek, B. (Eds.). (1983). *Understanding the multicultural experience in early childhood education.* Washington, DC: National Association for the Education of Young Children.

Schaller, M., Asp, C. H., Rosell, M. C., & Heim, S. J. (1996). Training in statistical reasoning inhibits the formation of erroneous group stereotypes. *Personality and Social Psychology Bulletin, 22,* 829–844.

Schaller, M., & Maass, A. (1989). Illusory correlation and social categorization: Toward an integration of motivational and cognitive factors in stereotype formation. *Journal of Personality and Social Psychology, 56,* 709–721.

Schaller, M., & O'Brien, M. (1992). "Intuitive analysis of covariance" and group stereotype formation. *Personality and Social Psychology Bulletin, 18,* 776–785.

Schofield, J. W. (1980). Complementary and conflicting identities: Images and interaction in an interracial school. In S. Asher & J. Gottman (Eds.), *The development of children's friendships*. Cambridge: Cambridge University Press.

Schofield, J. W. (1991). School desegregation and intergroup relations: A review of the literature. *Review of Education, 17*, 335–409.

Schofield, J. W. (1995). Promoting positive intergroup relations in school settings. In W. D. Hawley & A. W. Jackson (Eds.), *Toward a common destiny* (pp. 257–314). San Francisco: Jossey-Bass.

Schwartz, S. H. (1992). Universals in the content and structure of values: Theoretical advances and empirical tests in 20 countries. In M. Zanna (Ed.), *Advances in experimental social psychology* (Vol. 25, pp. 1–25). New York: Academic Press.

Schwartz, S. H., & Bilsky, W. (1990). Toward a theory of the universal content and structure of values: Extensions and cross-cultural replications. *Journal of Personality and Social Psychology, 58*, 878–891.

Sears, D. O. (1988). Symbolic racism. In P. A. Katz & D. A. Taylor (Eds.), *Eliminating racism: Profiles in controversy* (pp. 53–85). New York: Plenum.

Sears, D. O., & Allen, H. M., Jr. (1984). The trajectory of local desegregation controversies and whites' opposition to busing. In N. Miller & M. B. Brewer (Eds.), *Groups in contact: The psychology of desegregation* (pp. 124–155). New York: Academic Press.

Sears, D. O., & Citrin, J. (1985). *Tax revolt: Something for nothing in California*. Cambridge, MA: Harvard University Press.

Sears, D. O., & Funk, C. L. (1991). The role of self-interest in social and political attitudes. In M. Zanna (Ed.), *Advances in experimental social psychology* (Vol. 24, pp. 1–99). Orlando, FL: Academic Press.

Sears, D. O., & Kinder, D. R. (1971). Racial tensions and voting in Los Angeles. In W. Z. Hirsch (Ed.), *Los Angeles: Viability and prospects for metropolitan leadership*. New York: Praeger.

Sears, D. O., & Kinder, D. R. (1985). Whites' opposition to busing: On conceptualizing and operationalizing group conflict. *Journal of Personality and Social Psychology, 48*, 1141–1147.

Sears, D. O., & Lau, R. R. (1983). Inducing apparently self-interested political preferences. *American Journal of Political Science, 27*, 223–252.

Sears, D. O., Lau, R. R., Tyler, T. R., & Allen, H. M., Jr. (1980). Self-interest vs. symbolic politics in policy attitudes and presidential voting. *American Political Science Review, 74*, 670–684.

Secord, P. E., & Backman, C. W. (1964). *Social psychology*. New York: McGraw-Hill.

Shachar, H., & Amir, Y. (1996). Training teachers and students for intercultural cooperation in Israel. In D. Landis & R. S. Bhagat (Eds.), *Handbook of intercultural training* (pp. 400–443). Thousand Oaks, CA: Sage.

Sharan, S., & Shachar, H. (1988). *Language and learning in the cooperative classroom*. New York: Springer.

Sherif, M. (1966). *Group conflict and cooperation.* London: Routledge & Kegan Paul.

Sherif, M., Harvey, O. J., White, B. J., Hood, W. R., & Sherif, C. W. (1961). *Intergroup conflict and cooperation: The Robbers' Cave experiment.* Norman: University of Oklahoma Press.

Sherif, M., & Sherif, C. W. (1956). *An outline of social psychology* (2nd ed.). New York: Harper & Row.

Shirts, G. (1973). *BAFA–BAFA: A cross-cultural simulation.* Del Mar, CA: Simile 11.

Sidanius, J. (1993). The psychology of group conflict and the dynamics of oppression: A social dominance perspective. In W. McGuire & S. Iyengar (Eds.), *Current approaches to political psychology* (pp. 183–219). Durham, NC: Duke University Press.

Sidanius, J., Levin, S., & Pratto, F. (1996). Consensual social dominance orientation and its correlates within the structure of American society. *International Journal of Intercultural Relations, 20,* 385–408.

Sidanius, J., & Pratto, F. (1993). The inevitability of oppression and the dynamics of social dominance. In P. M. Sniderman, P. E. Tetlock, & E. G. Carmines (Eds.), *Prejudice, politics, and the American dilemma* (pp. 173–212). Stanford, CA: Stanford University Press.

Simpson, G. E., & Yinger, J. M. (1985). *Racial and cultural minorities: An analysis of prejudice and discrimination* (5th ed). New York: Plenum.

Skov, R. B., & Sherman, S. J. (1986). Information-gathering processes: Diagnosticity, hypothesis-confirmatory strategies, and perceived hypothesis confirmation. *Journal of Experimental Social Psychology, 22,* 93–121.

Skowronski, J. J., Carlston, D. E., & Isham, J. T. (1993). Implicit versus explicit impression formation: The differing effects of labeling and covert priming on memory and impressions. *Journal of Experimental Social Psychology, 29,* 17–41.

Slavin, R. E. (1977). *Student learning teams techniques: Narrowing the achievement gap between the races* (Report No. 228). Baltimore: Johns Hopkins University, Center for the Organization of the Schools.

Slavin, R. E. (1978). Student teams and achievement divisions. *Journal of Research and Development in Education, 12,* 381–387.

Slavin, R. E. (1985). Cooperative learning: Applying contact theory in desegregated schools. *Journal of Social Issues, 41,* 45–62.

Slavin, R. E. (1990). *Cooperative learning: Theory, research, and practice.* Englewood Cliffs, NJ: Prentice-Hall.

Slavin, R. E. (1991). *Student team learning: A practical guide to cooperative learning.* Washington, DC: National Education Association.

Slavin, R. E. (1992). Cooperative learning: Applying contact theory in the schools. In J. Lynch, C. Modgil, & S. Modgil (Eds.), *Cultural diversity in the schools* (Vol. II, pp. 333–348). London: Falmer Press.

Slavin, R. E. (1995). Cooperative learning and intergroup relations. In J. A. Banks & C. A. McGee Banks (Eds.), *Handbook of research on multicultural education* (pp. 628–634). New York: Macmillan.

Slavin, R. E., & Madden, N. A. (1979). School practices that improve race relations. *American Educational Research Journal, 16,* 169–180.

Sleeter, C. E. (1992). *Keepers of the American dream.* London: Falmer Press.

Sleeter, C. E., & Grant, C. A. (1987). Race, class, gender and disability in current
textbooks. In M. W. Apple & L. K. Christian-Smith (Eds.), *The politics of the
textbook* (pp. 78–110). New York: Routledge.

Smith, A. (1990). Social influence and antiprejudice training programs. In J. Edwards, R. S. Tisdale, L. Heath, & E. J. Posavic (Eds.), *Social influence processes and intervention* (pp. 183–196). New York: Plenum.

Smith, E. E., Shoben, E. J., & Rips, L. J. (1974). Structure and process in semantic
memory. *Psychological Review, 81,* 214–241.

Smith, E. J. (1991). Ethnic identity development: Toward the development of a
theory within the context of majority/minority status. *Journal of Counseling
and Development, 70,* 181–187.

Smith, E. R., & Lerner, M. (1986). Development of automatism of social judgments. *Journal of Personality and Social Psychology, 50,* 246–259.

Smith, H. J., & Tyler, T. R. (1997). Choosing the right pond: The impact of group
membership on self-esteem and group-oriented behaviors. *Journal of Experimental Social Psychology, 33,* 146–170.

Smock, P. J., & Wilson, F. D. (1991). Desegregation and the stability of white en-
rollments: A school level analysis, 1968–1984. *Sociology of Education, 64,*
278–292.

Sniderman, P. M., Tetlock, P. E., Carmines, E. G., & Peterson, R. S. (1993). The
politics of the American dilemma: Issue pluralism. In P. M. Sniderman, P. E.
Tetlock, & E. G. Carmines (Eds.), *Prejudice, politics, and the American dilemma* (pp. 212–236). Stanford: Stanford University Press.

Snyder, M. (1984). When belief creates reality. In L. Berkowitz (Ed.), *Advances
in experimental social psychology* (Vol. 18, pp. 247–305). New York: Academic Press.

Snyder, M. (1992). Motivational foundations of behavioral confirmation. In M.
Zanna (Ed.), *Advances in experimental social psychology* (Vol. 25, pp. 67–
114). Orlando, FL: Academic Press.

Snyder, M., & Haugen, J. A. (1994). Why does behavioral confirmation occur? A
functional perspective on the role of the perceiver. *Journal of Experimental
Social Psychology, 30,* 218–246.

Snyder, M., & Swann, W. B. (1978). Hypothesis-testing in social interaction. *Journal of Personality and Social Psychology, 36,* 1202–1212.

Snyder, M., Tanke, E. D., & Berscheid, E. (1977). Social perception and interpersonal behavior: On the self-fulfilling nature of social stereotypes. *Journal of
Personality and Social Psychology, 35,* 656–666.

Snyder, M., & White, P. (1981). Testing hypotheses about other people: Strategies of verification and falsification. *Personality and Social Psychology Bulletin, 7,* 39–43.

Spence, J. T., & Helmreich, R. L. (1978). *Masculinity and femininity.* Austin: University of Texas Press.

Srull, T. K. (1981). Person memory: Some tests of associative storage and retrieval models. *Journal of Experimental Psychology: Human Learning and Memory, 7,* 440–463.

Srull, T. K., Lichtenstein, M., & Rothbart, M. (1985). Associative storage and retrieval processes in person memory. *Journal of Experimental Psychology: Learning, Memory, and Cognition, 11,* 316–345.

Stahl, R. J. (Ed.). (1994). *Cooperative learning in social studies: A handbook for teachers.* Menlo Park, CA: Addison-Wesley.

Stangor, C., & Duan, C. (1991). Effects of multiple task demands upon memory for information about social groups. *Journal of Experimental and Social Psychology, 27,* 357–378.

Stangor, C., Lynch, L., Duan, C., & Glass, B. (1992). Categorization of individuals on the basis of multiple social features. *Journal of Personality and Social Psychology, 62,* 207–218.

Stangor, C., & McMillan, D. (1992). Memory for expectancy-congruent and expectancy-incongruent information: A review of the social and social developmental literatures. *Psychological Bulletin, 111,* 42–61.

Stangor, C., Sullivan, L. A., & Ford, T. E. (1991). Affective and cognitive determinants of prejudice. *Social Cognition, 9,* 359–380.

Stephan, W. G. (1978). School desegregation: An evaluation of predictions made in *Brown* vs. *The Board of Education. Psychological Bulletin, 85,* 217–238.

Stephan, W. G. (1985). Intergroup relations. In G. Lindzey & E. Aronson (Eds.), *Handbook of social psychology* (Vol. III, pp. 599–658). New York: Addison-Wesley.

Stephan, W. G. (1986). Effects of school desegregation: An evaluation 30 years after *Brown.* In L. Saxe & M. Saks (Eds.), *Advances in applied social psychology* (Vol. 3, pp. 181–206). New York: Academic Press.

Stephan, W. G. (1987). The contact hypothesis in intergroup relations. In C. Hendrick (Ed.), *Group processes and intergroup relations* (pp. 13–40). Beverly Hills, CA: Sage.

Stephan, W. G. (1991). School desegregation: Short-term and long-term effects. In H. J. Knopke, R. J. Norrell, & R. W. Rogers (Eds.), *Opening doors: Perspective on race relations in contemporary America* (pp. 100–118). Tuscaloosa: University of Alabama Press.

Stephan, W. G., Ageyev, V., Coates-Shrider, L., Stephan, C. W., & Abalakina, M. (1994). On the relationship between stereotypes and prejudice: An international study. *Personality and Social Psychology Bulletin, 20,* 277–284.

Stephan, W. G., & Rosenfield, D. (1978). The effects of desegregation on racial attitudes. *Journal of Personality and Social Psychology, 36,* 795–804.

Stephan, W. G., & Rosenfield, D. (1982). Racial and ethnic stereotypes. In A. G. Miller (Ed.), *In the eye of the beholder* (pp. 92–136). New York: Praeger.

Stephan, W. G., & Stephan, C. W. (1984). The role of ignorance in intergroup relations. In N. Miller & M. B. Brewer (Eds.), *Groups in contact: The psychology of desegregation* (pp. 229–257). New York: Academic Press.

Stephan, W. G., & Stephan, C. W. (1985). Intergroup anxiety. *Journal of Social Issues, 41,* 157–175.

Stephan, W. G., & Stephan, C. W. (1989a). After intermarriage: Ethnic identity among mixed heritage Japanese-Americans and Hispanics. *Journal of Marriage and the Family, 51,* 507–519.

Stephan, W. G., & Stephan, C. W. (1989b). Emotional reactions to interracial achievement outcomes. *Journal of Applied Social Psychology, 19,* 608–621.

Stephan, W. G., & Stephan, C. W. (1991). Intermarriage: Effects on personality, adjustment, and intergroup relations in two samples of students. *Journal of Marriage and the Family, 53,* 241–250.

Stephan, C. W., & Stephan, W. G. (1992). Reducing intercultural anxiety through intercultural contact. *International Journal of Intercultural Relations, 16,* 89–106.

Stephan, W. G., & Stephan, C. W. (1993). Cognition and affect in stereotyping: Parallel interactive networks. In D. M. Mackie & D. L. Hamilton (Eds.), *Affect, cognition, and stereotyping: Interactive processes in group perception* (pp. 111–136). San Diego: Academic Press.

Stephan, W. G., & Stephan, C. W. (1996a). *Intergroup relations.* Boulder, CO: Westview Press.

Stephan, W. G., & Stephan, C. W. (1996b). Predicting prejudice. *International Journal of Intercultural Relations, 20,* 1–18.

Stephan, W. G., Ybarra, O., & Bachman, G. (in press). Prejudice toward immigrants: An integrated threat theory. *Journal of Applied Social Psychology.*

Stern, L. D., Marrs, S., Cole, E., & Millar, M. G. (1984). Processing time and recall of inconsistent and consistent behaviors of individuals and groups. *Journal of Personality and Social Psychology, 47,* 253–262.

Stewart, E. (1966). The simulation of cultural differences. *Journal of Communication, 16,* 291–304.

Stewart, E., Danielian, J., & Foster, R. (1969). *Simulating intercultural communication through role playing.* Arlington, VA: HUMRRO Technical Report 69-7.

Stoskopf, A. L., & Strom, M. (1990). *Choosing to participate: A critical examination of citizenship in American history.* Brookline, MA: Facing History and Ourselves National Foundation.

Sumner, W. G. (1906). *Folkways.* Boston: Ginn.

Swann, W. B., Jr., & Ely, R. J. (1984). A battle of wills: Self-verification versus behavioral confirmation. *Journal of Personality and Social Psychology, 46,* 1287–1302.

Swim, J. K., Aiken, K. J., Hall, W. S., & Hunter, B. A. (1995). Sexism and racism: Old fashioned and modern prejudices. *Journal of Personality and Social Psychology, 68,* 199–214.

Tajfel, H. (1970, November). Experiments in intergroup discrimination. *Scientific American,* pp. 96–102.

Tajfel, H. (Ed.). (1978). *Differentiation between social groups: Studies in the social psychology of intergroup relations.* London: Academic Press.

Tajfel, H. (1981). *Human groups and social categories: Studies in social psychology.* Cambridge: Cambridge University Press.

Tajfel, H. (1982). *Social identity and intergroup relations.* Cambridge: Cambridge University Press.

Tajfel, H., & Turner, J. C. (1979). An integrative theory of intergroup conflict. In

S. Worchel & W. G. Austin (Eds.), *Psychology of intergroup relations* (pp. 33–47). Monterey, CA: Brooks/Cole.

Tajfel, H., & Turner, J. C. (1986). The social identity theory of intergroup behavior. In S. Worchel & W. G. Austin (Eds.), *Psychology of intergroup relations* (2nd ed.; pp. 7–24). Chicago: Nelson-Hall.

Thompson, L. (1993). The impact of negotiation on intergroup relations. *Journal of Experimental Social Psychology, 29,* 304–325.

Thomson, B. J. (1992). *Words can hurt you: Beginning a program of anti-bias education.* Reading, MA: Addison-Wesley.

Tolson, E., McDonald, S., & Moriarity, A. (1992). Peer mediation among high school students: A test of effectiveness. *Social Work in Education, 14,* 86–93.

Tougas, F., Brown, R., Beaton, A. M., & Joly, S. (1995). Neosexism: Plus ca change, plus c'est pareil. *Personality and Social Psychology Bulletin, 21,* 842–849.

Triandis, H. C. (1972). *The analysis of subjective culture.* New York: Wiley.

Triandis, H. C. (1975). Culture training, cognitive complexity, and interpersonal attitudes. In R. W. Brislin, S. Bochner, & W. J. Lonner (Eds.), *Cross-cultural perspectives on learning* (pp. 39–78). New York: Wiley.

Triandis, H. C. (1976). *Interpersonal behavior.* Monterey, CA: Brooks/Cole.

Triandis, H. C. (1994). *Culture and social behavior.* New York: McGraw-Hill.

Trope, Y., & Bassok, M. (1983). Information-gathering strategies in hypothesis-testing. *Journal of Experimental Social Psychology, 52,* 560–576.

Trope, Y., & Thompson, E. P. (1997). Looking for truth in all the wrong places? Asymmetric search of individuating information about stereotyped outgroup members. *Journal of Personality and Social Psychology, 73,* 229–241.

Turner, J. C., Brown, R. J., & Tajfel, H. (1979). Social comparison and group interest in ingroup favoritism. *European Journal of Social Psychology, 9,* 187–204.

Turner, J. C., Hogg, M. A., Oakes, P. J., Reicher, S. D., & Wetherell, M. S. (1987). *Rediscovering the social group: A self-categorization theory.* New York: Basil Blackwell.

Tyler, T. R., Degoey, P., & Smith, H. J. (1996). Understanding why justice procedures matter. *Journal of Personality and Social Psychology, 70,* 913–930.

U.S. Commission on Civil Rights. (1967). *Racial isolation in the schools.* Washington, DC: U.S. Government Printing Office.

U.S. Commission on Civil Rights. (1987). *The new evidence on civil rights on school desegregation.* Washington, DC: U.S. Government Printing Office.

Vanbeselaere, N. (1991). The different effects of simple and crossed categorizations: A result of the category differentiation process or of differential category salience? *European Review of Social Psychology, 2,* 247–278.

Vivian, J., Hewstone, M. J., & Brown, R. (1994). Intergroup contact: Theoretical and empirical developments. In R. Ben-Ari & Y. Rich (Eds.), *Understanding and enhancing education for diverse students: An international perspective.* Tel-Aviv: Bar-Ilan University Press.

Wagner, U., & Schonbach, P. (1984). Links between educational status and prejudice: Ethnic attitudes in West Germany. In N. Miller & M. B. Brewer (Eds.), *Groups in contact: The psychology of desegregation* (pp. 29–52). New York: Academic Press.

Watson, G. (1947). *Action for unity.* New York: Harper.

Weber, R., & Crocker, J. (1983). Cognitive processing in the revision of stereotypic beliefs. *Journal of Personality and Social Psychology, 45,* 961–977.

Webster, S. W. (1961). The influence of interracial contact on social acceptance in a newly desegregated school. *Journal of Educational Psychology, 45,* 292–296.

Weigel, R. H., & Howes, P. W. (1985). Conceptions of racial prejudice. *Journal of Social Issues, 41,* 117–138.

Weigel, R. H., Wiser, P. L., & Cook, S. W. (1975). The impact of cooperative learning experiences on cross-ethnic relations and helping. *Journal of Social Issues, 31,* 219–244.

Weiner, M. J., & Wright, F. E. (1973). Effects of undergoing arbitrary discrimination upon subsequent attitudes toward a minority group. *Journal of Applied Social Psychology, 3,* 94–102.

Weldon, D. E., Carlston, D. E., Rissman, A. K., Slobodin, L. F., & Triandis, H. C. (1975). A laboratory test of effects of culture assimilator training. *Journal of Personality and Social Psychology, 32,* 300–310.

Wilder, D. A., & Allen, V. L. (1978). Group membership and preference for information about others. *Personality and Social Psychology Bulletin, 4,* 106–110.

Wilder, D. A., & Shapiro, P. (1991). Facilitation of outgroup stereotypes by enhanced ingroup identity. *Journal of Personality and Social Psychology, 27,* 431–452.

Wilder, D. A., & Simon, A. F. (1996). Incidental and integral affect as triggers to stereotyping. In R. M. Sorrentino & E. T. Higgins (Eds.), *Handbook of social cognition* (Vol. 3, pp. 397–422). New York: Guilford Press.

Williams, J. E., & Morland, K. J. (1976). *Race, color, and the young child.* Chapel Hill: University of North Carolina.

Williams, R. M., Jr. (1947). *The reduction of intergroup tensions.* New York: Social Science Research Council.

Williams, R. M., Jr. (1964). *Strangers next door.* Englewood Cliffs, NJ: Prentice-Hall.

Williams, R. M., Jr. (1977). *Mutual accommodation: Ethnic conflict and cooperation.* Minneapolis: University of Minnesota Press.

Wilson, F. D. (1985). The impact of school desegregation on white public school enrollment. *Sociology of Education, 58,* 137–153.

Wilson, K. L. (1979). The effects of integration and class on black educational attainment. *Sociology of Education, 52;* 84–98.

Worchel, S. (1986). The role of cooperation in reducing intergroup conflict. In S. Worchel & W. G. Austin (Eds.), *Psychology of intergroup relations* (2nd ed.; pp. 288–322). Chicago: Nelson-Hall.

Word, C., Zanna, M. P., & Cooper, J. (1974). The nonverbal mediation of self-fulfilling prophecies in interracial interaction. *Journal of Experimental Social Psychology, 10,* 109–120.

REFERENCES   131

Wyer, R. S., Jr., & Martin, L. L. (1986). Person memory: The role of traits, group stereotypes, and specific behaviors in the cognitive representation of persons. *Journal of Personality and Social Psychology, 50,* 661–675.

Ybarra, O. J., & Stephan, W. G. (1994). Perceived threat as a predictor of stereotypes and prejudice: Americans' reactions to Mexican immigrants. *Boletín de Psicología, 42,* 39–54.

Zeichner, K. M. (1995). Preparing educators for cross-cultural teaching. In W. D. Hawley & A. W. Jackson (Eds.), *Toward a common destiny* (pp. 397–422). San Francisco: Jossey-Bass.

Ziegler, S. (1981). The effectiveness of cooperative learning teams for increasing cross-ethnic friendship: Additional evidence. *Human Organization, 40,* 264–268.

INDEX

Abalakina, M., 32
Aboud, F. E., 33–34, 60, 73, 83, 95
Abrams, D., 41
Achievement, cooperative learning groups and, 64–65
Acikgoz, K., 70
Ackerman, N., 24
Adelman, L., 41, 42
Adlerfer, C. P., 45
Administrators, 45–46
Affect. *See also* Mood
  creating positive, 50
  prejudice and, 26, 35
  stereotypes and, 14–17, 22, 23
African-Americans
  empathy of Whites for, 90–91
  equal-status relationships with Whites, 64–65
  friendships with Whites, 43
  historical relations with Whites, 55–56
  intercultural training programs and, 86
  prejudice and, 25, 26, 27, 34–35
  school desegregation and, 50–55, 56
  social identity and, 73–74
  stereotypes concerning, 2, 5, 7, 9–13, 19, 21, 34, 85, 86, 90–91
Ageyev, V., 32
Aggression, intergroup, 30, 46
Aiken, K. J., 35
Akin, T., 94
Allen, H. M., Jr., 26
Allen, V. L., 8, 29
Allison, S. T., 20, 83
Allport, F. H., 41
Allport, G. W., 24, 40, 41, 63, 87, 92, 100
Ambivalence-amplification theory, 27, 31, 35, 36, 39
American Dilemma, An (Myrdal), 93
Amir, Y., 43, 64
Andersen, S. M., 6

Anderson, J. R., 3
Anxiety, 31, 38, 96–97
Araki, C., 70
Armor, D. J., 53
Aronson, E., 42, 43, 45, 63, 64, 91, 93
Ashmore, R. D., 30–31, 60
Asian-Americans, 2, 5, 12, 24, 29, 85
Asp, C. H., 13, 84
Astin, A., 53, 83
Asuncion, A. G., 20, 83
Attitudes, xi, xiv. *See also* Contact theory; Prejudice
Authoritarianism, 47, 50
Authority figures, 29, 44–47. *See also* Administrators; Teachers
Aversive racism theory, 26, 31, 35, 36, 39

Bachman, G., 24
Backman, C. W., 24, 46
BAFA-BAFA, 68
Baker, S. M., 14
Banaji, M. R., 2, 6
Bandura, A., 100
Banks, C. A. M., x
Banks, J. A., ix–xii, 61, 62, 72–73, 90, 91, 94, 95, 101
Bargh, J. A., 5, 6, 20
Bashner, R. S., 20
Basso, K. H., 98
Bassok, M., 8
Beaton, A. M., 26
Behaviors, in network model of stereotypes, 4, 6
Behling, M., 101
Beliefs, xi, xiv, 8–10. *See also* Stereotypes
Benson, F. W., 45
Berscheid, E., 12
Bettencourt, B. A., 11, 44, 84
Bhawuk, D. P. S., 68

Bias
    cognitive, 13–14, 16, 87
    information processing, 91–92
    in labeling, 22, 85–86
    in perception, 84
Billig, M., 29
Bilsky, W., 94
Black, J. S., 68, 86
Blaming, 13–14, 84
Blanchard, F. A., 41, 42, 45, 47
Blaney, N., 42, 43, 45, 63, 64, 91, 93
Blatt, M. M., 66
Blumberg, R. G., 45
Bobo, L., 30
Bochner, S., 48, 96
Bodenhausen, G. V., 7, 9, 16
Borgida, E., 19, 43
Bovasso, G., 31
Bower, G. H., 14, 15
Bowers, V., 83
Braddock, J. H., II, 52–54, 72
Brady, M., 12
Brandt, M. E., 68
Branscombe, N. R., 95
Breckheimer, S. E., 60
Brekke, N., 43
Brewer, M. B., 37, 41–42, 44, 83, 84
Bridgeman, D. L., 64, 91
Brigham, J. C., 2, 34
Brislin, R. W., 22, 46, 68, 69, 86
Brown, R. J., 26, 29, 41, 44–45
Brown v. Board of Education, 50–55
Bruffee, K. A., 63
Burnstein, E., 42
Burton, J. W., 32, 69
Byrne, D., 87
Byrnes, D. A., 60, 83

Campbell, D. T., 30, 31
Canary, D. J., 96
Carillo, M. A., 21, 89
Carlisle, C. J., 13, 18
Carlston, D. E., 18, 22, 69, 86
Carmines, E. G., 7
Carpenter, S. L., 5
Carter, D. E., 45
Cash, T. F., 11
Cauce, A. M., 73, 95
Census Bureau, U.S., ix
Chaiken, S., 24
Chanowitz, B., 20
Characteristic features, in network model
    of stereotypes, 3–4, 5
Charity, 94
Charlton, K., 11
Chatel, D., 30

Chein, I., 41
Cherrie, C., 22
Children
    developmental phases of, 75
    optimal ages to employ social interac-
        tion techniques, 81–82
    social categorization by, 33–34, 38–39
    violation of others' rights by, 46
Citrin, J., 26
Civil Rights Movement, 50–55, 56
Clark, M. S., 14
Clegg, A. A., 94
Coates-Shrider, L., 32
Cognition
    cognitive bias and, 13–14, 16, 87
    in network model of stereotypes, 13–
        17
    training in, 83
Cohen, E. G., 21, 41–43, 45, 47, 63–65, 91,
        93, 95, 100–101
Cohen, S. P., 27, 69, 98
Cole, E., 10
Coleman, P. T., 71
Collett, P., 96
Commins, B., 90
Compassion, 94
Compunction theory, 27–28, 31, 35–36, 39
Conflict resolution skills, 69–71, 97–98
Contact, of ingroup with outgroup, 32, 35–
        36, 38
Contact hypothesis, 41–48, 50, 52, 92–93,
        100–101
Contact theory, 40–56. See also Prejudice
    contact hypothesis and, 40, 41–48, 50,
        52, 92–93, 100–101
    insights from, 55–56
    school desegregation and, 50–55, 56
    updated version of, 46–50
Contrast American exercise, 68
Converse, E., 24
Cook, S. W., 41–43, 46, 47, 52, 63, 64
Cooper, J., 12
Cooperation, 41–42, 43
Cooperative learning groups, 63–66, 91–92
Corbitt, E. M., 12
Coser, L., 30
Costrich, N.J., 11, 87
Council of the Great City Schools, ix
Cozarelli, C., 9
Crain, R. L., 52–54, 72
Crane, M., 43
Critical perspective, 93
Crocker, J., 11, 17, 19–21, 83, 87, 99
Cross, W. E., Jr., 73–74
Cross-cultural training programs, 67–69
Cross-cutting categories, 90

Cultural sensitizers, 68–69
Cupach, W. R., 96
Cushner, K., 22, 38, 69, 86

Danielian, J., 68
Dardenne, B., 8
Darley, J. M., 9, 19
Davidson, F. H., 66, 94
Davidson, M. M., 66, 94
Davidson-Podgorny, G., 42
Dawkins, M. P., 72
Day, H. R., 69
Deaux, K., 11
deDreu, C. K. W., 20
Defining features, in network model of stereotypes, 3, 5–7
Degoey, P., 29, 95
Del Boca, F. K., 30–31
Demographic characteristics, ix, 50
Desegregation. See School desegregation
Desforges, D. M., 42
DeTine, S. L., 45
Deutsch, M., 63, 65, 70, 71, 97
Devine, P. G., 5, 7, 14, 27, 28, 87, 88
DeVries, D. L., 63–65
Didactic programs, in intergroup relations, 59–63
Dignity, 94
Dill, K. E., 11
Dinnerstein, L., 62
Disciplinary actions, 72
Discrimination, 28
    incentives for nondiscriminatory behavior, 101
    injustice of, 98–99
    school policies concerning, 101
    social categorization and, 82, 83
Dishonesty, 10–11
Dispute resolution centers, 98
Diversity, as positive value, 94–95
Doob, L. W., 69
Dovidio, J. F., 14, 22, 26, 31, 64, 89, 93, 97
Doyle, A. B., 33–34, 60, 73, 95
Duan, C., 20, 82
Duckitt, J., 24
Dudley, B., 69–71, 97
Duncan, B., 7, 9
Dutta, S., 16

Eagly, A. H., 24, 32
Eaton, S. F., 51–54, 56
Edwards, K. J., 41–42, 44, 63–65
Effrein, E. A., 12
Egalitarianism, 92–93
Elliot, A. J., 27
Ellison, C. G., 53

Ely, R. J., 21
Empathy, 90–91
Epstein, J. A., 42
Epstein, J. L., 72
Erber, R., 15, 19, 64
Eshel, S., 46
Esses, V. M., 16, 24, 30–32, 97
Ethnic identity, 44–45, 95
Ethnocentrism, of children, 34
Evans, M., 9, 13
Evans, N., 14
Exemplars
    defined, 3
    in network model of stereotypes, 5
Expectancy-confirmation sequence, 7–13
    effects of expectancies on perceptions, 9–12, 19–20
    self-fulfilling prophecies and, 12–13, 17, 20–21, 88–89
    stereotype-based expectancies and, 87–89
    trait information in, 7–9, 10–11, 13, 19–20
Extroversion, 8–9

"Facing History and Ourselves" curriculum, 66–67, 94
Fairness, 94
Falender, V. J., 12
Family, 2, 54, 72
Farber, J., 27
Farley, R., 53
Favoritism, 29
Fazio, R. H., 12
Fear
    as cause of prejudice, 96–97
    integrated threat theory and, 29–33, 37–38
    systematic desensitization and, 35
Fein, S., 20, 91
Feinstein, L., 11, 87
Fine, M., 66, 67, 90, 94
Finlay, C. A., 90
Fischer, G. W., 82
Fisher, R., 70, 98
Fiske, S. T., 14, 17, 19, 64, 91
Fleming, J. H., 19
Ford, T. E., 32
Fordham, S., 73
Foster, R., 68
Freibergs, V., 16
Frey, D., 26
Friendship
    authority figure support for, 45
    cross-racial, 43, 45, 53
    stereotypes and, 2

Fulero, S., 9, 13
Funk, C. L., 26

Gaertner, S. L., 22, 26, 31, 64, 89, 93, 97
Gangs, 30
Gayle, M., 15
Gehrke, E. M., 7, 87
Generalizations, 1–2, 42
Genser, L., 94
Gerard, H. B., 52
Gersho, B. F., 13, 18
Gilbert, D. T., 13, 19
Glass, B., 82
Glass, D.C., 27, 93, 97
Gonzales, A., 42
Gonzales, N. A., 73, 95
Goodman, M. E., 33
Grant, C. A., 61–63, 72
Grant, G. W., 62
Grant, P. R., 11, 44
Gray, D. B., 60
Greathouse, S. A., 11
Greece, 70
Green, K., 52, 53
Greenberg, J., 30
Gross, P. H., 9
Group labels
    in network model of stereotypes, 3–4, 6,
        14–15, 20
    personalizing outgroup members and,
        83–84
Group similarities, 87
Gudykunst, W. B., 30, 68
Gurin, P., 93

Haarman, A., 15
Haddock, G., 16, 24, 30–32, 97
Hall, W. S., 35
Hallinan, M. T., 42, 72
Hamilton, D. L., 10, 13, 15, 16, 18, 87
Hammer, M. R., 68
Handbook of Research on Multicultural Edu-
    cation (Banks & Banks), x
Hannah, D. B., 11, 19, 83, 87
Harackiewicz, J. M., 42
Hardin, C., 6
Harding, J., 41
Harrington, H. J., 41, 42, 44, 83, 84
Harris, M. J., 12
Harris & Associates, 54
Harvey, O. J., 22, 63, 89
Haslam, A. S., 29
Hass, R. G., 14, 27
Hastie, R., 11
Hate speech, 46
Haugen, J. A., 12
Hauserman, N., 101

Hawes, J. A., 52, 53
Hawley, W., 54
Heim, S. J., 13, 84
Helmreich, R. L., 6
Hemsley, G. D., 10, 11
Henderson-King, E. I., 20
Hepburn, C. A., 20, 43
Hertz-Lazarowitz, R., 63, 64
Hewstone, M., 11, 31, 44–45, 83, 84, 90
Higgins, E. T., 16
Hilton, J. L., 10, 19, 20
Hinton, G. E., 3
Hirt, E. R., 7, 87
Hispanics, 19, 46–47
Hixon, G., 19
Hoffman, E., 42
Hogg, M. A., 29
Hohn, R. L., 60
Holmes, J. G., 11, 44
Holubec, E. J., 63, 91
Honesty, 10–11
Hood, W. R., 22, 63, 89
Hoover, D. W., 12
Hopkins, N., 11
Howes, P. W., 47
Hulgus, J. F., 69
Hunter, B. A., 35

Impressions, changing, 11
Individualized contact, 43–45
Ingroups. See also Outgroups
    contact with outgroups, 32, 35–36, 38.
        See also Contact theory
    defined, 5
    knowledge of outgroup, 33, 37
    prejudice of outgroup toward, 36–38, 74
    social identity theory and, 29, 95
Inservice teachers, 62–63
Integrated threat theory, 29–33, 37–38
Intercultural training programs, 86
Intergroup interaction
    importance of, 96–97
    interpersonal interaction versus, 44–45,
        49–50
Intergroup relations, 58–102. See also Con-
    tact theory; Prejudice; Stereotypes
    anxiety in, 31, 38
    development of intergroup attitudes,
        33–34, 38–39
    prior intergroup conflict, 32
    techniques for improving, 58–71
Intergroup relations programs
    conflict resolution techniques and, 69–
        71, 97–98
    cooperative learning groups, 63–66,
        91–92
    cross-cultural training programs, 67–69

development of intergroup relations skills and, 81, 96–99
didactic, 59–63
in educational settings, 58–67, 71–76, 80–102
issues related to, 71–76, 81, 92–95
moral development training programs, 66–67
in noneducational settings, 67–71
recommendations for, 80–102
school policies and, 45–46, 71–73, 101
social culture of schools and, 81, 100–102
social identity and, 73–76, 84–86, 95
social information processing and, 80–81, 82–92
teacher training for, 101–102
values and identity issues in, 81, 92–95, 98–99
Interpersonal interaction, 44–45, 49–50
Inter-team competition, 42
Introversion, 8–9
Isen, A. M., 14, 22
Isham, J. T., 18
Islam, M. R., 31, 90
Israel, 64
Ivey, A., 60, 99

Jackman, M. R., 43
Jackson, L. A., 11
Jahoda, M., 24
James, W., 9
Jaspars, H., 84
Jigsaw classroom, 63
John, O. P., 10, 19, 20, 38, 44, 64, 83
Johnson, D. W., 41, 63–65, 69–71, 91, 97–98
Johnson, R. C., 76
Johnson, R. T., 41, 63–65, 69–71, 91, 97–98
Johnston, L., 9, 83, 87
Jones, E. E., 13
Jones, J. M., 85
Jost, J. T., 2
Judd, C. M., 90
Judice, T. N., 21, 89
Justice, 94, 98–99

Kagan, J., 46
Kamfer, L., 70, 88, 99
Kanungo, R. N., 16
Katz, I., 14, 27, 93, 97
Katz, J. H., 60, 99
Katz, P. A., 33
Kehoe, J. W., 60
Kelley, H. H., 18
Kellison, C., 98
Kelman, H. C., 24, 69, 98
Kendall, F. E., 62

Kidder, L., 11, 87
Kiger, G., 60, 83
Kinder, D. R., 25, 26
King, G., 16
Kirkland, S., 30
Klatzky, R., 6
Kleinfeld, J., 62
Kohlberg, L., 66, 94
Kramer, G. P., 16
Krueger, J., 44
Kulik, J., 11
Kumar, A. P., 11
Kunda, Z., 11
Kutner, B., 41

Labeling
bias in, 22, 85–86
in network model of stereotypes, 3–4, 6, 14–15
stereotypes and, 2, 3–4, 6, 14–15
Landis, D., 22, 38, 68, 69
Langer, E. J., 20
Lau, R. R., 26
Lepper, M. R., 19, 42
Lerner, M., 6
Levin, S., 28
LeVine, R. A., 30, 31
Lewin, K., 1
Lewis, L. L., 11
Lewis, S., 20
Leyens, J., 8
Leyens, J. P., 20
Li, F., 5
Lichtenstein, M., 10, 20, 87
Linville, P. W., 82
Locksley, A., 20, 43
Lockwood, J., 90
Logan, B., 98
Longshore, D., 42
Lopez, G. E., 93
Lord, C. G., 19, 42
Lowrance, R., 22
Lucido, D. J., 27
Lucker, G. W., 42, 47, 64, 65
Lynch, L., 82
Lyon, D., 30

Maass, A., 13
Mackie, D. M., 13, 15, 16, 18, 20, 83
Madden, N. A., 72
Magnusson, D., 70, 71, 97
Mahan, J. M., 63
Mahard, R., 52, 72
Major, B., 9, 99
Majority groups. See Ingroups
Malle, B. F., 28
Mann, J., 22, 64, 89

Marachek, J., 11, 87
Marmurek, H. V. C., 10, 11
Marrs, S., 10
Martin, L. L., 9
Maruyama, G., 41
Maslow, A. H., 87
Mason, J. A., 42
Mass media, stereotypes and, 2
Masson, C. N., 45
Mayer, J. D., 15
McArthur, L. Z., 18, 82
McClelland, J. L., 3
McClendon, M. J., 43
McConahay, J. G., 54, 97
McCrae, R., 42
McDill, E. L., ix
McDonald, S., 70
McFarlin, D. B., 9
McGarty, C., 29
McGee Banks, C. A., 72
McGregor, J., 59, 60, 90, 91
McGrew, P. L., 69
McMillan, D., 10, 20
McPartland, J., 52–54
Mediators
    in conflict resolution, 70–71, 97–98
    of contact, 48, 49, 56
Meehan, M. E., 15
Memory, bias in, 13–14, 16
Mendenhall, M., 68, 86
Meneses, L. M., 13, 18
Merton, R. K., 7
Milich, R., 12
Millar, M. G., 10
Miller, A. B., 69
Miller, N., 41–42, 44, 63, 83, 84
Miller, R. L., 52, 53
Minority groups. See Outgroups
Mladinic, A., 32
Monteith, M. J., 27, 28, 88
Mood. See also Affect
    ability to process information and, 16
    positive, 91–92
    positive traits and, 18
    in processing of stereotypes, 15–16, 22
    stereotype change and, 23
Moral development training programs,
    66–67
More than Meets the Eye (Bowers & Swan-
    son), 83
Moriarity, A., 70
Morland, K. J., 34
Mulholland, A., 11
Multicultural education, 61–63, 91–92
    curriculum and, 72–73, 95, 101
    defined, x

dimensions of, x–xi
empathy and, 90–91
goals of, ix–x, 61–62
training teachers in, 62–63, 72
Murrell, A., 22, 64, 89
Mydral, G., 25, 93

Nagda, B. A., 93
Nagoshi, C., 76
Narot, R., 72
National Council for the Social Studies
    Task Force, 61–62
Native Americans, 22, 98
Natriello, G., ix
Nedler, B. F., 13, 18
Negative traits, 18–21
Neidenthal, P. M., 14
Nelson, R. O., 60
Neosexism, 26
Network model of stereotypes, 3–17
    affect and cognition in, 14–17, 22, 23
    cognitive biases and, 13–14
    components of, 3–5
    expectancy-confirmation sequence and,
        7–13
    group labels in, 3–4, 6, 14–15, 20
    implications of, 7–13
    processing in, 5–7
Neuberg, S. L., 12, 20, 21, 89
Newcomb, T., 24
Nichols, R. L., 62
Nieto, S., 93, 101
Nisbett, R. E., 13, 20
Nodes
    defined, 3
    in network model of stereotypes, 3–5, 6,
        14
Noordhoff, K., 62
Norvel, N., 42

Oakes, P. J., 29
O'Brien, M., 13
Ogbu, J., 73
Okihiro, G. Y., 24
Oleson, K. C., 11
Olson, J. M., 24
Omoto, A. M., 19
Orfield, G., 51–54, 56
Organizational culture, 100–101
Ortiz, V., 20
Osgood, C. E., 32
Ostrom, T. M., 5
Outgroups. See also Ingroups
    avoidance of, 31
    contact with ingroups, 32, 35–36, 38.
        See also Contact theory

defined, 5
friendships and, 43
ingroup knowledge of, 33, 37
personalizing members of, 83–84
prejudice toward ingroup, 36–38, 74
social identity theory and, 29

Pallas, A. M., ix
Palomares, U., 98
Parents, 2, 54, 72
Parsons, M. A., 54
Pascale, L., 11, 87
Patchen, M., 32, 72
Patnoe, S., 63, 91, 93
Pavelchak, M. A., 14, 91
Peace, 94
Peace Corps, 68
Pearce, D., 53
Pedersen, P., 46, 74
Peichert, J. A., 52, 53
Perception
    biased, 84
    effect of expectancies on, 9–12, 19–20
Peres, Y., 46
Personality traits, 47, 50
Person consequences, of contact, 48, 49
Person factors, 47–50
Peterson, R. S., 7
Pettigrew, T. F., 21, 24, 40, 42, 51, 53, 55,
    56, 84
Phinney, J. S., 46
Phobias, 35
Pomare, M., 22, 64
Ponterotto, J. G., 74
Positive traits, 17–18
Posner, M. I., 14
Post, D. L., 18
Power, 32–33, 97
Powers, D. A., 53
Pratto, F., 20, 28, 93
Prejudice, 24–39. *See also* Contact theory
    affect and, 26, 35
    African-Americans and, 25, 26, 27, 34–35
    ambivalence-amplification theory of, 27,
        31, 35, 36, 39
    Asian-Americans and, 24, 29
    aversive racism theory of, 26, 31, 35, 36,
        39
    changing, xiii, xiv, 34–39, 62, 93
    compunction theory of, 27–28, 31, 35–
        36, 39
    defined, 24
    development of intergroup attitudes
        and, 33–34, 38–39
    fear as cause of, 96–97
    injustice of, 98–99

integrated threat theory of, 29–33,
    37–38
of minority group toward majority
    group, 36–38, 74
school policies concerning, 101
social categorization and, 33–34, 38–39,
    82
social dominance theory of, 28–29, 31,
    36, 39
social identity theory of, 29, 37
symbolic racism theory of, 25–26, 31,
    34–35, 36, 39
theories of, 25–33, 38–39, 97
Whites and, 24–25, 26, 27, 34–35
Preservice teachers, 62–63, 72
Preston, E., 19
Program for Complex Instruction, 65
Programmed learning, 86
Proshansky, N., 41
Pysczynski, T., 30

Quattrone, G. A., 82
Queller, S., 15, 16

Racism
    aversive, 26, 31, 35, 36, 39
    egalitarianism and, 92–93
    injustice of, 99
    social dominance theory and, 28–29, 31,
        36, 39
    social identity and, 73–74
    symbolic, 25–26, 31, 34–35, 36, 39
Ramsey, P. G., 62, 90
Ramsey, S. L., 42
Rasinski, K. A., 11
Reichel, L. D., 13, 18
Reicher, S. D., 29
Reimers, D. M., 62
Religious identity, 95
Respect, 94
Rholes, W. S., 16
Riordan, C., 42
Rips, L. J., 3
Rissman, A. K., 22, 69, 86
Rogers, T. W., 60
Rogers-Croak, M., 44, 84
Rokeach, M., 35, 88
Role playing, 60, 68, 90–91
Root, M. P. P., 75
Roper, S., 21, 42, 47, 93
Rose, T., 13
Rosell, M. C., 13, 84
Rosenblatt, A., 30
Rosenfeld, D., 5, 33, 34, 42, 45, 47, 55, 64,
    65
Ross, M. H., 70

Rossell, C. H., 53, 54, 56
Rothbart, M., 9, 10, 13, 19, 20, 38, 44, 64, 83, 87
Rotheram, M. J., 46
Rothman, A. J., 6
Rouhana, N. N., 69
Routh, D. A., 11
Roy, P., 96
Roye, W. J., 45
Rumelhart, D. E., 3
Ruvolo, C. M., 10, 87

Sagar, H. A., 9
Sagiv, L., 67
Salovey, P., 15, 82
Sanbonmatsu, D. M., 13
Sapir, C., 64
Sarocho, O. N., 62
Schaller, M., 13, 84
Schofield, J. W., 9, 10, 12, 46, 52, 71–72, 101
Schonbach, P., 47
School desegregation, 50–55, 56
School policies, 45–46, 71–73, 101
Schroth, H. A., 13, 18
Schwartz, S. H., 67, 94
Sears, D. O., 25, 26, 30, 97
Secord, P. E., 24, 46
Sedikides, C., 5
Segregation by group, 71–72
Self-esteem, 37, 47, 50, 64, 84, 95
Self-fulfilling prophecy, stereotypes and, 7, 12–13, 17, 20–21, 88–89
Sexism, 26, 28–29, 99
Shachar, H., 64
Shakespeare, William, 16
Shapiro, P., 12
Sharan, S., 64
Sheppard, L. A., 16
Sherif, C. W., 22, 24, 63, 89
Sherif, M., 22, 24, 30, 63, 89
Sherman, S. J., 7, 8, 10, 13, 87
Shirts, G., 68
Shoben, E. J., 3
Sidanius, J., 28, 29, 93
Sikes, J., 42, 43, 45, 63, 64, 91, 93
Simon, A. F., 91
Simon, L., 30
Simpson, G. E., 24
Situational context, for contact, 48, 49
Situational factors, 41–46, 55–56
Skov, R. B., 7, 8
Skowronski, J. J., 18
Slavin, R. E., 41, 42, 45, 63–65, 72, 91, 101
Sleeter, C. E., 61–63
Slobodin, L. F., 22, 69, 86
Smith, A., 60, 90
Smith, E. E., 3

Smith, E. J., 74
Smith, E. R., 6
Smith, H. J., 29, 95
Smith, S. S., 42
Smock, P. J., 53
Snapp, M., 43, 45, 63, 91, 93
Sniderman, P. M., 7
Snyder, C. R. R., 14
Snyder, M., 7–8, 12, 19, 87, 88
Social categorization process
  cross-cutting categories, 90
  prejudice and, 33–34, 38–39, 82
  race in, 33–34, 38–39
  social information processing and, 82–83, 89–90
  stereotypes and, 2, 5–6, 22
  superordinate categories and, 89
Social dominance theory, 28–29, 31, 36, 39
Social identity theory, 29, 37, 73–76
  intergroup relations and, 73–76, 81, 84–86, 92–95, 98–99
  mixed heritage and, 75–76
  stages of identity development and, 74–75
Social information processing, 80–81, 82–92
  biased labeling and, 22, 85–86
  biased perceptions and, 84
  cross-cutting categories and, 90
  empathy and, 90–91
  group similarities and, 87
  personalizing outgroup members and, 83–84
  positive moods and outcomes and, 91–92
  social categories and, 82–83, 89–90
  stereotype-based expectancies and, 87–89
  subjective culture and, 38, 86
  superordinate categories and, 89
Socialization, xiv, 27–28
Societal consequences, of contact, 48, 49
Societal context, of contact, 48, 49
Societal factors, 46–47, 48
Socioeconomic status, 9, 42–43, 64–65
Soloman, L. K., 18
Solomon, S., 30
South Africa, 70, 99
Spence, J. T., 6
Spencer, S. J., 91
Spero, J., 45
Spodek, B., 62
Srull, T. K., 10, 20, 87
Stahl, R. J., 91
Stallworth, L. M., 28
Stangor, C., 10, 20, 32, 82
Status, 9, 32–33, 42–43, 64–65, 97

Stephan, C. W., 2, 14, 19, 30–32, 38, 41–43, 45, 50, 59, 60, 63, 64, 75, 76, 91, 93, 96–97
Stephan, W. G., 2, 5, 14, 19, 24, 30–34, 38, 41, 42, 45, 47, 50, 51, 55, 59, 60, 65, 75, 76, 90, 91, 96–97
Stereotype-disconfirming evidence, 10, 19–21
Stereotypes, 1–23, 50
　activation of, 5–7, 14–15, 27–28, 88
　affect and, 14–17, 23
　African-Americans and, 2, 5, 7, 9–13, 19, 21, 34, 85, 86, 90–91
　Asian-Americans and, 2, 5, 12, 85
　categorization as basis of, 2, 5–6, 22
　changing, xiii, xiv, 11, 17–23, 64, 93
　counteracting, 16–17, 88
　detrimental effects of, 1–2, 88
　expectancies and, 87–89
　generalizations versus, 1–2
　Hispanics and, 19, 46–47
　injustice of, 98–99
　Native Americans and, 22
　nature of, 1–2
　negative, 21, 27–28, 31–32, 38, 82–83, 93
　network model of, 3–17
　school policies concerning, 101
　self-fulfilling prophecy and, 7, 12–13, 17, 20–21, 88–89
　student reliance on, 2
　subtypes and, 11, 21–22
　Whites and, 2, 5, 9, 10, 12–14, 19, 21, 34, 85
Stern, L. D., 10
Stewart, E., 68
Stoskopf, A. L., 66
Straus, J., 53
Stroessner, S. J., 15, 16
Strom, M., 66
Students of color, statistics on, ix
Subjective culture, 38, 86
Subtypes, 11, 21–22
Sullivan, L. A., 32
Sumner, W. G., 31
Superordinate categories, 89
Susser, K., 16
Swann, W. B., 7–8, 12
Swann, W. B., Jr., 19, 21
Swanson, D., 83
Swim, J. K., 35
Symbolic racism, 25–26, 31, 34–35, 36, 39
Symbolic sexism, 26
Systematic desensitization, 35

Tajfel, H., 29, 46, 73, 82, 84
Tanke, E. D., 12
Tate, W. F., 62, 63, 72

Taylor, S. E., 17
Teachers. See also Intergroup relations programs
　ethnic identities of students and, 44–45
　expectations for students, 12
　intergroup relations training, 101–102
　multicultural education training, 62–63, 72
　social identity theory and, 29
　support for intergroup contact, 45–46
Teixeira, R. A., 72
Testa, M., 9
Tetlock, P. E., 7
Thibodeau, R., 63
Thomas, J. A., 69
Thompson, E. P., 9
Thompson, L., 60
Thomson, B. J., 90
Threats, 29–33, 37–38, 97
Tolson, E., 70
Tougas, F., 26
Tracking, 72
Training
　cognition, 83
　cross-cultural, 67–69
　intercultural, 86
　moral development, 66–67
　multicultural education, 62–63, 72
　teacher, 62–63, 72, 101–102
Traits
　evaluation of, 85–86
　expectancies concerning, 7–9, 10–11, 13, 19–20
　links to negative, 18–21
　links to positive, 17–18
　in network model of stereotypes, 3–4, 6, 7–9, 10–11, 13, 14–15, 19
Trent, W., 53
Triandis, H. C., 22, 33, 38, 60, 69, 86
Trope, Y., 8, 9
Turkey, 70
Turner, J. C., 29, 73, 82, 84
Turner, R., 24
Tyler, R. B., 14
Tyler, T. R., 26, 29, 95

U.S. Commission on Civil Rights, 51, 53–54

Values, xi
　American, 94
　diversity, 94–95
　egalitarianism, 92–93
　in intergroup relations programs, 81, 92–95, 98–99
　prejudice and, 26
　subjective culture and, 86
　universalistic, 94

Vanbeselaere, N., 90
VanLeeuven, M. D., 42
Veeder, M., 30
Venter, J. L., 70, 88, 99
Verkuyten, M., 45
Virdin, L. M., 21, 89
Vivian, J., 44–45
von Hippel, W., 10

Wackenhut, J., 14, 27, 93, 97
Wagner, U., 47
Walen, S. R., 101
Wann, D. L., 95
Watson, G., 41
Weber, J., 98
Weber, R., 11, 19–21, 83, 87
Webster, S. W., 45
Weigel, R. H., 42, 43, 47, 63, 64
Weiner, M. J., 60
Weisman, C., 53, 54
Weldon, D. E., 22, 69, 86
West, S. C., 42
Wetherell, M. S., 29
White, B. J., 22, 63, 89
White, P., 19
White flight, 53–54
Whites
    empathy with African-Americans, 90–91
    equal-status relationships with African-
        Americans, 64–65
    friendships with African-Americans, 43
    historical relations with African-
        Americans, 55–56

impact of school desegregation on,
    53–55
intercultural training programs and,
    86
prejudice and, 24–25, 26, 27, 34–35
social identity and, 73–75
stereotypes concerning, 2, 5, 9, 10, 12–
    14, 19, 21, 34, 85
Wilder, D. A., 8, 12, 29, 91
Williams, J. E., 34
Williams, R. M., Jr., 41, 45–47, 63
Wilson, F. D., 53, 54
Wilson, G., 72
Wilson, K. L., 52
Wilson, S., 98
Wiser, P. L., 42, 43, 63, 64
Worchel, S., 41, 42
Word, C., 12
Worth, L. T., 20, 83
Wright, F. E., 60
Wyer, R. S., Jr., 7, 9

Ybarra, O. J., 24, 30
Yinger, J. M., 24
Yong, M., 22
Yoshida, T., 68
Yzerbyt, V. Y., 20

Zanna, M. P., 12, 16, 24, 30–32, 97
Zeichner, K. M., 72
Ziegler, S., 64
Zuwerink, J. R., 27, 28, 88

ABOUT THE AUTHOR

Walter G. Stephan received his Ph.D. in psychology from the University of Minnesota in 1971. He has taught at the University of Texas at Austin, the University of Hawaii, and New Mexico State University. He has published numerous articles on intergroup relations, including studies of school desegregation, prejudice, stereotyping, and techniques of improving intergroup relations. His books include *School Desegregation* (edited with Joe Feagin, 1980), *Two Social Psychologies* (with Cookie Stephan, 1985, 1990), and *Intergroup Relations* (with Cookie Stephan, 1996). In 1996 he won the Otto Klineberg award (along with co-author Marina Abalakina-Paap), given by Division 9 of the American Psychological Association for the best paper published during that year on intercultural relations.